After 1992
The United States of Europe

In the wake of Margaret Thatcher's resignation and her championship of unfettered national sovereignty, Ernest Wistrich argues that the changes of 1992 will precipitate the transformation of the European Community into a full political and economic union, organized according to federal principles. He finds evidence for this in the reforms already agreed and in the history of the Community's development.

In a thorough examination of its responsibilities in the monetary, economic, social and cultural spheres, the author traces the Community's progress towards its objective of European Union. He recommends further reforms that are needed to attain this objective and to ensure the competitiveness of the new Union within a world of rapid technological, economic and political change. Wistrich goes on to suggest ways in which national cultural diversities can be preserved within a federal structure, even as a common European identity is forged. In particular he introduces the principle of restricting federal powers to those matters that need common solutions and management, thus ensuring maximum autonomy and self-government in local communities and regions. He also makes novel proposals for integrating most of the rest of Europe within the emerging European Union and for a new special relationship with the Soviet Union.

This book, which includes a foreword by the Rt Hon. Lord Jenkins, the former President of the European Commission, provides a lucid argument for the federalist case. Of particular interest to decision-makers in commerce and industry, and to politicians, the book will also be of value to all those interested in the economic, social and political implications of the single European market.

The author

Ernest Wistrich is Vice-President of the International European Movement, and was until 1986 Director of the European Movement in Britain. He has also edited *The European, Facts, Into Europe*, and *New Europe*, and has written many articles on European topics. He was appointed CBE in 1973 for services to the European cause.

After 1992
The United States of
Europe

Revised Edition

Ernest Wistrich

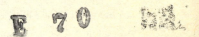

London and New York

First published 1989 by Routledge
11 New Fetter Lane, London EC4P 4EE

Reprinted 1989, 1990
New in paperback revised edition 1991

Simultaneously published in the USA and Canada
by Routledge
a division of Routledge, Chapman and Hall, Inc.
29 West 35th Street, New York, NY 10001

© 1989, 1991 Ernest Wistrich

Typeset by LaserScript Limited, Mitcham, Surrey
Printed in Great Britain by
Biddles Ltd, Guildford and King's Lynn

British Library Cataloguing in Publication Data

Wistrich, Ernest
    After 1992 : the United States of Europe.
    1. European community countries. Economic integration
    I. Title
    337.1'42

ISBN 0-415-06457-0 (Pbk)
ISBN 0-415-04451-0

Library of Congress Cataloging-in-Publication Data
Wistrich, Ernest.
    After 1992: the United States of Europe/Ernest Wistrich.
        p. cm.
    Includes bibliographical references.
    ISBN 0-415-04451-0
    ISBN 0-415-06457-0 (Pbk)
    1. European cooperation. 2. European federation. 3. European
Economic Community countries. I. Title
D1060.W57   1990
    341.24'-dc20   89-10928
                                                           CIP

341.242
W817

Contents

Acknowledgements

The writing of this book was suggested by the Federal Trust for Education and Research which, since the 1940s, has been the principal British think tank on European integration. To help me in this task the Federal Trust organized a seminar in 1988 to discuss some of the issues to be covered by the book. My special thanks go to Dr. Roy Pryce and Mr. John Pinder, director and chairman respectively of the Federal Trust, for their detailed comments and suggestions for the improvement of the manuscript. I am grateful to my friend Douglas Gardner, a lifelong journalist and committed European, for going through the text and helping me to make it more readable. I dedicate the book to my wife Enid who, on hearing that I was to write it at home, pointed out that she had married me for better or for worse but not for lunch. Nevertheless, as an academic and author in her own right, her advice and unfailing support sustained me during the many months it took to draft it.

ERNEST WISTRICH

Foreword

Ernest Wistrich was for seventeen years until 1986 the Director of the British section of the European Movement. Subsequently he was editor of the journal *The European*. A teenager refugee from eastern Europe, who received most of his education in Poland but was here in time to spend four wartime years in the RAF, he has been the key organizer of support, over the most crucial years, for Britain's integration into western Europe.

Often those who are organizational linchpins do not greatly concern themselves, beyond a general commitment, with details of the policies they are promoting. Even senior staff officers are not expected to expatiate much on military geo-policies, and Chief Whips mostly accept the policy judgements of their Prime Ministers, at any rate until they tell them that maybe it is time to resign.

Mr. Wistrich, however, was never a director who just buried his head in the bureaucratic details of circulars and conferences. I vividly recollect how at European meetings he vigorously and encouragingly nodded his head if he agreed with the point one was making, and if not, not. One reason was that, as this book abundantly reveals, he had the whole raft of European issues more at his finger-tips than did the speakers for whom he organized meetings, and had very trenchant views upon the issues, and no doubt upon the speakers as well.

This is a vivid and lucid book. It is at once informative and proselytizing. Ernest Wistrich is an unapologetic federalist to an extent that is today unusual in Britain (although not in most other Community countries). He does not whisper behind a cupped hand, as is often done, that federalism may be a proclaimed ideal but is not to be taken too seriously. On the other hand he is a flexible federalist. He is devoted to the principle of 'subsidiarity', by which Brussels should 'only exercise those responsibilities which cannot be more effectively dealt with at state, regional, or local level'. And he constantly applies himself to practical problems, so that his recipes for advance spring naturally out of recognizable problems rather than being imposed in accordance with some pre-determined blueprint.

He is also a non-hectoring proselytizer. His clearly expressed beliefs can be taken or left, without there being any need for somebody of contrary persuasion to get irritated with them, and without their getting in the way of the calm exposition of a great deal of useful information, mainly about the history of the Community and of the federalist idea, both on the continent and in Britain.

At the end the author permits himself a swoop of imagination. At the European elections of 2014, with a greatly enlarged Community into which the whole of an opened up eastern Europe has been drawn, Gabriella Bosconi (presumably of Italy) is re-elected President, while her running-mates, Patrick Antrim, the first protestant Taoiseach of a united Ireland, and Krystyna Krolik, the Polish Foreign Minister who persuaded the Russians to agree to enlargement to the east, are respectively chosen (all by direct election) as presiding officers of the Council of Ministers and of the European Parliament. Thus in a single leap is he able to bring together his pan-Europeanism, his federalism, his belief in leading roles for women, and his optimism about 'European' solutions for some of the problem areas of the continent. It requires faith to see all this happening in twenty-five years, but it has become a great deal more possible in the past five years, both because of the recovery of dynamism in the west and because of the prospect of changes in the east, than was the case in 1984.

ROY JENKINS
5 March 1989

Chapter one

The logic of 1992

Over the last half a century there has been greater change than over the preceding 500 years. The technological revolution has radically altered the nature of the world. The indiscriminate exploitation of natural resources and the uncontrolled use of them in some countries is having a global effect. Our common environment and the world's climate are under serious threat. Nuclear accidents, like Chernobyl, could make large parts of our planet uninhabitable for thousands of years. Nuclear weapons threaten the very survival of humanity, were they ever to be used. The massive growth of international trade and its accompanying huge capital flows, and the emergence of multinational corporations, with annual turnovers often in excess of the gross national products of independent countries, have made the whole world economically interdependent. As a result countries that try to isolate themselves by erecting barriers against the outside pay a heavy price in economic stagnation and backwardness, while the rest of the world moves ahead.

These dramatic changes in the nature of global society have thrown up new problems that can no longer be tackled by individual countries merely looking after their own interests. Unfettered national sovereignty is obsolete, and economic and political independence is giving way to growing interdependence between nation states. The major task for the world today is to devise policies to deal with global problems and create appropriate political structures to ensure that the policies are put into effect. The same applies to individual continents or major regions within them that are affected by common problems. Amongst these, for instance, pollution, disease, crime, and terrorism know no frontiers and can no longer be tackled by individual countries in isolation, but require international solutions.

If total independence and unfettered sovereignty of nation states is becoming outdated, how should the world be organized? Merging individual countries into larger states with common governments is no answer. Most nations wish to preserve their distinct identities, languages, and cultures. At the same time as democracy and active citizen participation grows, so does resentment against over-centralized national governments and distant authority exercised over people's daily lives. Local communities and regions within countries demand devolution of power so that they can deal with their problems at their level, instead of leaving it to faceless national bureaucrats, less aware of and sensitive to local needs and wishes.

The federal path

The only flexible answer to these seemingly conflicting trends is the adoption of federal solutions to accommodate them. The essence of federalism lies in the decentralization of power wherever needs can be satisfied at lower levels of government, closer to the citizen. Although federations take many different forms, generally they have emerged to unite separate states in a way in which powers exercised at federal level are confined to those that need common solutions and management. Most federal constitutions guarantee maximum autonomy and self-government to the component parts of the federation. The general principle is that federal government can only exercise those responsibilities which cannot be effectively fulfilled by lower tiers of government.

The European Community was founded to deal with the changing political and economic world and has advanced quite far along the federal road towards a European Union, which is its explicit objective. Its legal status stems from a constitution based on the treaties setting up the Community and from their subsequent amendments. The constitution and Community laws are binding on member states. The European Community is governed by an independent executive in the form of the European Commission. This is answerable to a directly elected European Parliament which has powers to dismiss it. Community laws, which take precedence over national legislation, are formulated by the Commission and, after being subjected to formal consultation by the European Parliament, are enacted by the Council of Ministers representing member governments.

The rapidly changing world has created for the European Community and its member countries new challenges which require common action. That is why the Community is constantly evolving and acquiring new responsibilities and powers. The latest reform to the original treaties has dealt with the need for further economic integration of the Community, due to be implemented by the end of 1992. But already in 1988 a major debate has started on the next steps to follow the latest reforms. It is the purpose of this book to examine progress already made and recommend further reforms that will be necessary to attain the Community's declared objective of full union.

A common economic area

What is the current stage of progress? For all practical purposes, by the end of 1992 national frontiers between the twelve members states of the European Community will disappear. People, goods, services, and capital will move as freely between Glasgow and Naples, Copenhagen and Lisbon, or Dublin and Athens as between London and Manchester, Hamburg and Munich, or Paris and Lyons. That is the effect of the Single European Act negotiated between the twelve governments in Luxembourg in 1985 and ratified by all the national parliaments by 1987. The objective is to create a single European economy that is more dynamic, faster growing, creating millions of new jobs and able to compete on more equal terms with the USA and Japan.

When the Treaty of Rome established the European Economic Community in 1958 one of its objectives was to set up a common market without customs barriers, primarily to improve the living standards of its citizens. The creation of the Common Market had dramatic results. Between 1958 and 1972 the economies of the six members states of the Community grew much faster than that of the USA, the world's richest country. Britain, more prosperous than any of the Six when they started, had been overtaken by them all except Italy by the time she joined the Community fifteen years later. The progressive removal of the customs barriers and the development of closer economic relations between member states stimulated growth and accelerated the growth of living standards throughout the Community.

Following the oil crisis in 1973 and the subsequent recessions, progress in Europe slowed down and even halted. Yet the European Community's principal competitors, the USA, Japan, and the emerging industrial economies of the Far East, continued to forge ahead. Europe's record on productivity, innovation, inflation, unemployment, and new job creation was poor. Increasingly their products priced European goods even out of Europe's own domestic markets, let alone in the rest of the world. Relative impoverishment stared Europe in the face and something had to be done.

Albert–Ball Report

What had gone wrong? Various studies were undertaken. One of the most important was commissioned by the European Parliament. The resulting Albert–Ball Report (Albert and Ball 1983), was published in 1983 after a wide canvass of opinions amongst leading businessmen, government officials and academics throughout the European Community. It found that Europe had been sacrificing its future prosperity for the present, by spending money on current consumption

3

instead of modernizing and investing for growth. We had a tariff-free common market, but other barriers to trade within the Community were being erected. Instead of acting together, each member country operated on its own.

The Report showed that, whereas the EC's economy grew at 4.6 per cent per annum between 1960 and 1973, this fell to 2.3 per cent between 1973 and 1980. During the period of its rapid expansion the Community was able to maintain full employment and create millions of new jobs, many filled by migrant workers from outside the Community; but between 1973 and 1980 employment inside the EC actually decreased by three million, although in the USA it increased by fifteen million. Consequently unemployment rose much faster than in the USA. During the same 1973–80 period private and public consumption, as a share of the gross domestic product, rose by 6 per cent, whereas investment fell by 20 per cent. The rate of energy investment, for example, as a percentage of GDP, was two to three times lower than in the USA and Japan. By 1982 public expenditure in the Community – largely owing to a dramatic increase in social security payments to the unemployed – exceeded 50 per cent of GDP compared with 35 per cent in the USA and Japan. Between 1973 and 1981 industrial output in the Community rose by only 8 per cent compared with 16 per cent in the USA and 26 per cent in Japan.

In response to the economic crises of the 1970s, instead of uniting to safeguard their futures, each country pursued its own protective policies, and this led to serious monetary disorders with incessant exchange rate fluctuations. The effect was to inhibit intra-Community trade as exporters were denied stable markets for their products. The common market in agricultural products remained fragmented by positive or negative levies at frontiers which raised or lowered prices. There was no genuine common market for orders placed by public authorities, who favoured national suppliers. More barriers to free trade were being erected as new national regulations and standards conflicted with those of neighbouring countries.

To overcome the growing crisis individual countries tried to find national solutions to their problems. Yet, as at least 50 per cent of external trade was with each other, the economies of member countries became increasingly interdependent. Uncoordinated action could not solve problems which affected them all. Studies undertaken for the Report clearly demonstrated that isolated action by individual countries were bound to fail, but concerted action at Community level was much more likely to succeed. As the Report put it: 'Any country wishing to go it alone in pursuit of growth is bound to lose. Any country which, having put its house in order, agrees to go for growth with the others and according to rules reflecting the collective interest, is sure to gain by this action.' A clear example of this conclusion was provided between 1981 and 1983 when the French Socialist government, at the start of President Mitterrand's first term of office, tried to go for growth on its own. Within two years the resulting inflation and a balance of payments crisis forced that government to abandon its independent course.

Cost of barriers

The cost of the divisions between member countries was dramatic. Although the Common Market established a customs union without tariff barriers, goods moving between members' countries faced obstacles as formidable as before. Widely differing VAT rates meant that complicated refunds and payments were demanded at border crossings. Divergent national product standards, technical regulations and conflicting business laws prevented goods legally sold in one country from being exported to others. Administrative formalities involving massive paperwork, red tape, and border checks resulted in high and unproductive costs. So did interminable delays in crossing internal Community frontiers.

The most authoritative estimate of the cost of the divided Community was given in a 1988 report on the *Cost of Non-Europe* (Cecchini 1988) prepared at the request of the European Commission by an expert committee under the chairmanship of Paolo Cecchini. Their research was based on the most up-to-date scientific analysis, many individual studies, and an industrial survey involving some 11,000 enterprises across the Community. Their conclusions put the overall cost of existing barriers at about Ecu 200 billion (£130 billion). This was equivalent to about 5 per cent of the Community's Gross Domestic Product.

The elements making up the total were revealing. Based on interviews with some 500 firms in several Community countries, the administrative costs of customs formalities for private firms were estimated at 2 per cent of the value of the goods traded. The smaller the company, the higher the cost, preventing many from exporting altogether. Huge queues of trucks awaiting clearance at border crossings added further costs. A comparison of two truck trips of 1,200 kilometres – one within the United Kingdom and one between London and Milan – showed that the first took thirty-six hours whereas the second (excluding time lost in crossing the Channel) took fifty-eight hours. This represented a difference in transport costs of over 50 per cent. In addition the cost to public authorities of administering the customs formalities was estimated at between Ecu 500–1,000 million (£335–670 million).

Then there is the cost of national public purchasing policies that discriminate in favour of domestic suppliers. In fact, in the vast majority

5

of cases public procurement is awarded solely to national suppliers. Purchases controlled by the public sector – that is by central and local government, their agencies and monopoly-type enterprises – accounted for Ecu 530 billion (£350 billion) in 1986 or about 15 per cent of the Community's gross domestic product. This was more, incidentally, than the total value of intra-Community trade, which amounted to Ecu 500 billion. As a result of this protectionism against intra-Community competition the public sector generally pays more for the goods than it needs to. In 1986 the total cost of national protection in the field of public procurement was estimated at some Ecu 21.5 billion (£14.5 billion).

Differing technical regulations, standards, testing, and certification procedures are also a major barrier to freer trade. Technical regulations are laid down by national laws to provide health, safety, and environmental protection. Standards are set for products by various national standardization bodies. Trade is inhibited when one country refuses to recognize another's certificates and demands the application of its own tests. Entry can be barred to goods whose standards do not conform to those of the importing country. Such barriers inhibiting trade are significant in the case of telecom equipment, cars, foodstuffs, pharmaceuticals, and building products. In the case of these products the cost of the restrictive practices is estimated at Ecu 3.5 billion (£2.36 billion) for telecom equipment, Ecu 2.6 billion (£1.75 billion) for cars, between Ecu 500 million and Ecu 1 billion (£335–650 million) for foodstuffs, and Ecu 1.7 billion (£1.14 billion) for building products.

Differences in regulations affecting financial services, including banking, insurance, exchange controls, and operations in stocks and shares, had similarly limited trade and added substantially to costs. The removal of regulatory barriers and the abolition of exchange controls would probably cut costs by some Ecu 22 billion (£15 billion). And removing existing barriers relating to telecom and other business services would ultimately lead to savings of some Ecu 9 billion (£6 billion).

Finally there is the whole field of research and development, especially in technology. The Albert–Ball Report pointed out that Europe's total expenditure on research and development was close to that of the USA and double that spent in Japan. Yet in the early 1980s eight out of ten personal computers sold in Europe came from America and nine out of ten video-recorders came from Japan. The main reason for this has been the fragmentation of the research and development effort in Europe with each country pursuing its own policies, duplicating research, and often developing products that could not be sold to their neighbours.

All these restrictions to trade had to go if Europe was to become competitive again. This much was clear to all the European Community governments. But if genuine economic recovery was to be achieved much more needed to be done. The growing interdependence between the economies of member states meant that common action had to take the place of uncoordinated national policies pursued in isolation. Trading barriers were not the only obstacles. Major differences in indirect taxation needed to be reduced and frequent exchange rate fluctuations replaced by long-term currency stability. This signalled the need for much more co-ordinated economic policies. Many other changes were also essential; amongst them the removal of remaining restrictions on the movement of people and their right to work anywhere in the Community in their chosen occupations and professions.

The Cockfield Plan

To meet the challenge, the vice-President of the European Commission, Lord Cockfield, presented a White Paper (EC Commission 1985) to member governments in March 1985. This proposed the virtual removal of all internal Community barriers to the free movement of people, goods, services, and capital, completing the internal market and creating an economic area without frontiers by 1992. The White Paper listed some 300 measures which had to be enacted within a strict timetable.

The proposals covered the removal of non-tariff barriers such as customs posts, and immigration and passport controls, harmonizing public health standards, abolishing national transport controls, approximating arms and drugs legislation, removing all technical barriers to trade and harmonizing technical standards, liberalizing capital movements, approximating indirect taxation including VAT and excise duties, fixing minimum standards for goods and services and their mutual recognition, encouraging Community-wide public purchasing, abolishing remaining obstacles to the free movement of professions and labour, and establishing a common market in services in banking, insurance, transport, and communications.

Novel procedures were suggested. Instead of trying to harmonize everything to achieve uniformity throughout the Community, as in the past, the Commission recommended that wherever full harmonization was not essential there should be mutual recognition of national standards which met minimum common criteria, with goods lawfully manufactured and marketed in one member state being allowed free entry into other member states. The same principle was proposed for a general recognition of diplomas and qualifications for the professions.

7

The Single European Act

The proposals contained in the White Paper were approved by the Heads of Governments at their European Council meeting in Milan in June 1985, and it was decided that there should be an intergovernmental conference to negotiate the necessary amendments to the existing treaties. The conference took place at the end of 1985 in Luxembourg. It negotiated the Single European Act (EC Commission 1986) which, after ratification, came into force in 1987. Apart from measures required to complete the Internal Market, the Act also dealt with some of the recommendations made by the European Parliament on the achievement of a full European Union.

The Single European Act covered three main areas. The first defined new policy objectives. The second dealt with the decision-making and legislative processes. The third extended the Community's responsibilities to foreign policy and security matters.

The new policy objectives dealt with the completion of the internal market, the convergence of economic and monetary policies, improving living and working conditions, strengthening economic and social cohesion by reducing disparities between regions and particularly by helping the least-favoured regions, strengthening research and technological co-operation and development, preserving, protecting, and improving the quality of the environment, advancing health standards and promoting a more rational use of natural resources.

The system of qualified majority voting in the Council of Ministers was extended. The criteria agreed were that the adoption of general principles of new policies still required unanimous approval, but measures to implement them would be taken by qualified majority voting. The votes are weighted between member states according to their population: France, Germany, Italy, and the UK have ten votes each, Spain has eight, Belgium, Greece, The Netherlands and Portugal five each, Denmark and Ireland three each, and Luxembourg two votes. A qualified majority is represented by a minimum of fifty-four votes out of a total of seventy-six.

Legislative powers of the European Parliament were increased. Where the Council acts by qualified majority the Parliament can amend or reject Council decisions. Unanimous agreement in the Council is needed to overrule rejections or amendments submitted by the Parliament. Applications for membership of the European Community and association agreements with third countries also require parliamentary approval. The Commission's powers to implement rules laid down by the Council were more clearly defined. Powers of the European Court of Justice were also extended to cover cases submitted by the staff of European institutions.

Finally the Single European Act stipulates that member governments should jointly formulate and implement a European foreign policy and achieve closer co-operation on questions of European security. This codifies the existing practice of Political Co-operation but extends it to political and economic aspects of security. It also establishes a political secretariat to assist the Ministers of Foreign Affairs and the European Commission, which becomes fully associated in these fields. The European Parliament is kept fully informed and its views on foreign and security policies are to be taken into consideration.

Economic benefits

The Single European Act marked a major step forward in the process of European integration. It removed the log-jam that had built up through the failure of governments to take decisions that were not unanimous. It ended years of stagnation and relative economic decline. The Act furthermore recognized the logic of an integrated market which would not endure unless it also offered tangible measures for progress towards a full European economic and political union to which member governments had repeatedly committed themselves.

The completion of the Internal Market by the end of 1992 promises major economic benefits in the medium term. Consumers will be much better off. Economies of scale, improved efficiency, new patterns of competition and increased innovation will enable commerce and industry to reduce costs substantially. The Cecchini Report estimates that the integration of the market will trigger a major relaunch of economic activity, adding on average 4.5 per cent to the European Community's gross domestic product. It will also deflate consumer prices by an average of 6.1 per cent, improve the balance of public finances by an average of 2.2 per cent of GDP and boost the Community's external position by about 1 per cent of GDP. Some 1.8 million new jobs will be created reducing the jobless total by about 1.5 per cent. In the longer term further gains are likely from the self-sustaining effect of reduced production costs and improvements in productivity. These are estimated to result in a rise of up to 7.5 per cent in GDP and an increase in employment by up to 6 million new jobs.

As the Single European Act recognizes in its many additional provisions, completion of the Internal Market alone will not secure the many benefits that are expected. First, governments cannot pick and choose the measures which suit them and block those that they do not like. Approximation of VAT rates and excise taxes, co-ordination of economic policies, and stabilizing currency fluctuations all form an integral part of the whole strategy. Unless they are all achieved there will be no unified market and the expected benefits will not be realized.

9

Beyond the Act

The objectives of the Act, furthermore, are not ends in themselves. They represent merely one further step towards the Community's basic objective of full European Union. This process will necessitate growing convergence of the economies of the member states. Monetary stability remains fragile so long as the Community operates with twelve currencies. If full Economic and Monetary Union is to be achieved there will have to be common management of the European economy and a single European currency.

We also have to consider the extraordinary technological revolution now proceeding and the massive resources needed for research and development to compete with the technologically more advanced USA and Japan. This calls for a European strategy and much more substantial private and public financial resources. There has to be much greater rationalization of research and development in Europe, and the Community must also match the public procurement record of the US and Japanese governments in the field of high technology. This should apply as much to defence equipment as to non-military products and processes.

It is clear that the removal of internal frontiers and economic convergence could exacerbate social and regional inequalities, placing the weaker members of society and the more backward regions at even greater disadvantage than at present. To avoid this, economic integration has to be accompanied by parallel measures in social, regional, and environmental policies. The Community would not survive if it allowed some parts to enrich themselves at the expense of the weaker and poorer regions. Cohesive policies and solidarity must be the hallmark of progress to union, or it will never be accepted by those who feel themselves vulnerable and the Community would fall apart.

Further integration, with increasing concentration of powers at Community level, raises the question of democratic accountability. Those who already complain about the excessive power of national governments, view with concern proposals for removing power even further away into the hands of European bureaucrats. There has to be an entirely new approach to democratic accountability. If anything, there is a case for more devolution of powers from the centre, from national governments to the regions and from the regions to local communities, which know much better what their needs are. There is a case for a much more rational division of responsibilities between the different levels of government and greater democratic accountability of each tier. Such rationalization becomes more urgent with the growth of responsibilities at European Community level.

Europe in the world

Finally there is Europe's role in the world. In 1987 the European Community had a population of 320 million compared with 275 million in the USSR, 234 million in the USA, and 119 million in Japan. Europe's gross domestic product amounted to Ecu 380 billion (£255 billion) compared with Ecu 370 billion (£250 billion) for the USA and Ecu 200 billion (£135 billion) for Japan. The Community's share of world trade, according to GATT figures, was 18 per cent as against the United States' 17 per cent and Japan's 9 per cent. As these figures demonstrate, the European Community is an economic giant, potentially equal to the other economic super-powers. Politically, however, Europe does not speak with a single voice and accordingly has little influence when it comes to defending its interests.

In the field of security and defence Europe relies on the protection of the USA but it does not participate in American negotiations with the USSR over the defence of Europe. Yet European security is vitally dependent on relations with the Soviet bloc. Even on issues of economic co-operation the Community as such has not until recently spoken with the Soviet Union.

With the largest share of world trade, Europe's prosperity is more dependent on peace, stability, and economic progress in the rest of the world than other major powers. This concern is already reflected in the aid effort of the European Community which, at 40 per cent of all aid to the Third World, exceeds the combined total of aid from the USA, the USSR, and Japan. Yet much more needs to be done to reverse the growing disparity in wealth between north and south. Massive international debts incurred by developing countries cannot be repaid. Interest alone, paid to the richer countries, often exceeds aid received from them. Basic natural resources of our planet are being dangerously depleted and we all face global ecological disasters unless joint action is taken at world level.

Europe has a vital part to play on the world scene and must provide itself with the means and instruments to do so. War and economic chaos affecting so much of our planet mirrors Europe's own experience earlier this century. The means by which the countries of the European Community turned their backs on their strife-ridden past, made war between them unthinkable, and revived their economies together, could provide important lessons for other parts of the world. In the long run it could become a blueprint for the way in which the entire world might govern itself.

For or against the United States of Europe

However, before all these things can happen, the European Community will have to transform itself into, what Winston Churchill in his speech in Zürich in 1946 described as 'a kind of United States of Europe'. But will this happen? Is there a sufficient political will to make it happen? A major debate on this issue was triggered off in 1988, following a speech delivered by Commission President Jacques Delors to the European Parliament in July of that year. He declared his conviction that, as a consequence of the Single European Act, within ten years 80 per cent of economic legislation – and maybe even fiscal and social legislation – will be of Community origin. His assessment was not an isolated one. German Chancellor Kohl declared after the Hanover Summit in February 1988 that European Union was no longer a distant vision, and Belgian Premier Martens declared his expectation that the United States of Europe was finally within reach. Their views have been echoed by French President Mitterrand, Spanish Premier Gonzales, and several Italian statesmen.

Has Europe got a choice? According to Mrs. Thatcher, we certainly have. She explicitly rejected any idea of a United States of Europe and offered against it her vision of a European Community based on willing and active co-operation between independent and sovereign states. Her views, clearly expressed in a speech delivered in Bruges in September 1988, provide a perfect example of a head of a member government who is totally opposed to the transformation of the existing Community into a European federation, whether it is described as a European Union or the United States of Europe. Her speech therefore deserves a close analysis and critique.

At the start one needs to accept, fully and at face value, Mrs. Thatcher's clear commitment to continued British membership of the present European Community. She put it unequivocally in these terms: 'Britain does not dream of an alternative to the European Community, of some cosy isolated existence on its fringes. Our destiny is in Europe, as part of the Community.' The statement has a double significance. First, it implicitly accepts the level of integration already achieved including all transfers of national sovereignty to Community institutions that have already taken place. Second, it contains a rejection of any second-class status to which Britain could become relegated if she did not take full part in the Community's evolution.

Mrs. Thatcher set out her guidelines for the future in these terms:

> Willing and active cooperation between independent sovereign states is the best way to build a successful European Community. To try to suppress nationhood and concentrate power at the centre of a European conglomerate would be highly damaging and would jeopardise

the objectives we seek to achieve. Europe will be stronger precisely because it has France as France, Spain as Spain, Britain as Britain, each with its own customs, traditions and identity. It would be folly to try to fit them into some sort of indentikit European personality.

This attitude demonstrates a confusion between two separate issues. One concerns the transfer of responsibilities from national to Community levels. The other deals with national identity. The whole history of the Community, including the latest Single European Act, has been concerned with the transfer of those responsibilities from national to Community levels that member states have agreed require common management. And every consecutive Act or declaration made by member states, since the Community's inception, reiterates the commitment to greater unity and therefore to the Community's evolution into some form of union with common responsibilities, powers, and institutions. At no stage has it ever been suggested that the Community has reached its final form and that the existing treaties represent its fixed constitutional limits. Indeed the commitment to the Community's continued evolution towards European Union is explicitly stated in the Single European Act, only recently signed by Mrs. Thatcher's government and ratified by the British Parliament.

The other issue raised is that of the loss of national identity as Europe unites. It shows a profound misunderstanding of the whole process of European integration on the federal lines which have guided it since its inception. Not only have the national identities of the large countries, named by Mrs. Thatcher, never been under threat, but indeed those she did not name, which have been part of the Community for more than thirty years, have not only safeguarded their national customs, traditions, and identities, but have actually enhanced their voice and influence outside their borders. What heed would other countries have, for instance, given to the views of totally independent Belgium, Holland, or Luxembourg compared to the influence they actually exercise within the European Community. Through their votes and rotating presidencies their opinions count for very much more than they ever did on their own. The same indeed applies to all member states, as Lord Cockfield explained in his address to the Swiss Institute of International Affairs in Zürich in October 1988: 'The Community is based not on a loss of sovereignty but on a pooling of sovereignty, on its exercise jointly in the common good rather than its exercise separately – often selfishly and to the detriment of other people.'

At the same time, in an article in the *Sunday Telegraph*, on the question of losing identity Mr. Edward Heath put it even more bluntly:

What nonsense it also is to talk about the indentikit European. The United Kingdom has existed for several centuries. Can anyone convince me that they can't tell a Scot, a Welshman or an Irishman from an Englishman? And in the United States, that they can't tell a Texan from an East Coaster, or a Louisianan from a Chinatown San Franciscan? And what of this conglomerate? Do we damn the United States or Canada or Australia as conglomerates? Of course not.

Indeed, if the United Kingdom has not, over the centuries, managed to submerge the identities of the nations composing it, how much more unlikely is it that the ancient nations of Europe with their separate languages and cultures would disappear?

Whilst Mrs. Thatcher expressed herself in favour of Europe speaking with one voice on many great issues, she does not believe that this requires power to be centralized in Brussels or decisions to be taken by an appointed bureaucracy. Who then is to speak on behalf of Europe? The European Commissioners, while appointed by member states, are hardly bureaucrats but the governing executive of the European Community. They are political appointees, with their executive role spelt out in the treaties, answerable to the European Parliament but only able to operate within laws enacted by the ministers of the member states. As to her criticism of excessive centralization and bureaucracy, she forgets that the object of Community institutions is to cut down on national bureaucracies by getting rid of conflicting and contradictory national regulations and replacing them by common, simple, and clear regulations equally applicable in all member states.

She then championed the dispersal of power and decisions away from the centre and asserted that 'we have not successfully rolled back the frontiers of the state in Britain, only to see them re-imposed at European level with a European super-state exercising a new dominance from Brussels'. Her declarations in favour of decentralization sit oddly with her administration's contrary record of centralization in Britain, described in chapter 7. Be that as it may, she probably referred to deregulation and privatization in which Britain has been leading. Yet most of the responsibilities of the Community are those that would otherwise have had to have been handled by national governments and could not have been completely given up. Mrs. Thatcher's attack was presumably directed more narrowly at measures of social cohesion and proposed legislation on the rights of workers in enterprises. This very much reflects her hostility to trade unions and her idiosyncratic view that there is no such thing as society but only individuals, views which are not shared in most other European countries. This interpretation was confirmed by her comments on the European issue during the October 1988 Conservative Party Conference when she contrasted her vision of a Europe free of government interference with what she described as the interventionist attitude of those who want to build a socialist Europe.

Her next assertion was that 'the Treaty of Rome itself was intended as a charter for economic liberty'. This claim distorts the basic aims of the Treaty. Its explicitly declared objectives are to lay the foundations of an ever closer union among the peoples of Europe and ensure the economic and social progress of their countries by common action to eliminate the barriers that divide Europe. A further essential objective is the constant improvement of the living and working conditions of people, and the reduction of differences in wealth between the regions. Economic liberty, but within a framework of Community law, is implied by that part of the Treaty which deals with the removal of obstacles between countries by concerted action to guarantee steady expansion, balanced trade, and fair competition.

Her earlier outburst against the idea of a Central European Bank was followed by a more muted approach in her Bruges speech. Her priorities in the monetary field were free movement of capital, abolition of exchange controls, a free market in financial services, and a greater use of the Ecu. Only when these were achieved would she consider any further moves. The paradox of her championship of these measures is that they involve a greater loss of national sovereignty then most moves that had hitherto taken place in the economic sphere. Her government has not, however, as yet proposed the abolition of the Bank of England or of the economic powers wielded by her Chancellor of the Exchequer. But clearly twelve separate national banking institutions cannot control monetary policy at Community level. It is the latter that must regulate the market, manage the emerging European currency, and co-ordinate the economies of its member states.

There is another factor which she overlooked. The abolition of exchange controls and free movement of capital have major implications for the more vulnerable economies of member states. The tendency, as in Britain, is for wealth to flow to the richer areas, and, if the differences between richer and poorer regions are not to grow, compensating measures in the regional and social spheres are essential. That is the whole purpose of the Single European Act's sections on social policy and on economic and social cohesion which complement those on the internal market and its monetary capacity. The achievement of a fully integrated internal market would never have been agreed without a framework of economic, regional, and social policies that could guarantee its cohesion.

Although in favour of economic liberty with minimum regulation, Mrs. Thatcher backtracked on the Single Act's commitment to create an area without internal frontiers and with full freedom of movement of goods and people. As she put it: 'of course we must make it easier for goods to pass through frontiers. Of course we must make it easier for our people to travel throughout the Community. But . . . we cannot totally abolish frontier controls if we are to protect our citizens and stop the movement of drugs, of terrorists, of illegal immigrants.' Yet the movement of terrorists or illegal immigrants between Britain and Ireland cannot be controlled. Indeed travellers between the two countries, including Northern Ireland, that hotbed of terrorism, do not require passports or other forms of identity and they enjoy the full freedom of movement that is intended for the Community as a whole. As to the control of drugs, closer co-operation between national police forces and enforcement agencies would be much more fruitful and less costly then the maintenance of internal frontiers. Of course frontier controls for imports, and people coming from outside the Community, would have to continue.

Mrs. Thatcher dismissed all talk of 'utopian goals' and ranged herself fully on the side of General de Gaulle. As she put it during a broadcast interview in July 1988: 'I really was very much in agreement with de Gaulle that this is a Europe of separate countries working together.' She clearly shares de Gaulle's concept of a 'Europe des Patries' and his view that independence and national sovereignty must not be compromised or shared. This similarity of attitudes could also stem from the dominance which both leaders gained whilst in power in their countries. One explanation could be that advanced by Sir John Boyd Orr, the eminent British scientist, in his essay on *Federalism and Science* published in 1940 (Boyd Orr 1940). Noting the reluctance of some statesmen to delegate sovereignty he suggested that 'the psychologist should try to find reason for this prejudice ... It is probable that the leaders identify the state with themselves and feel that the loss of sovereign power would be a loss of their personal power.'

De Gaulle's rejection of supranationality led to a period of virtual stagnation in the Community's development between 1965 and 1969 when de Gaulle resigned. But here the comparison with Mrs. Thatcher's intentions to arrest the Community's progress to union is unlikely to apply. France under de Gaulle was the dominant power within the Community of the Six and no progress was possible without French consent. Britain is not central to the Community of the Twelve, being both a latecomer and as a country economically less significant than her French and German partners. Mrs. Thatcher's clout would be limited to exercising her veto only where unanimity is required for further progress. Should she press her opposition too strongly she might find other member states willing to contemplate a way to bypass Britain altogether.

Recognizing that some member states might be reluctant to move to European Union, the European Parliament, in its Draft Treaty (European Parliament 1984), made provision for such an eventuality. The Parliament proposed that the Union would come into effect if ratified by a majority of the member states whose populations totalled at least two thirds of the whole Community's population. Those countries not joining the Union could, however, retain with the Union all those relations which they enjoyed within the European Community. Indeed, such a solution, as suggested in chapter 8, might well accommodate some existing and future potential members who, for various reasons such as neutrality for instance, would find it difficult to become full members of a Union responsible for its own foreign and defence policies.

What would Britain's reaction be if faced with a determined move towards European Union by most of her Community partners with the possible exception of Denmark? If the intention to do so were to be made explicit to the British government, offering it an option to join or retain its current Community relationship on the margins of the proposed Union, a serious dilemma would confront the British. The heavy price that Britain paid for not joining the Community at its inception is not forgotten. More recent experience shows that, when faced with a determined majority in the Community, the British government went along with the majority. The best example was the Milan Summit meeting in 1985 which, following the European Parliament's Draft Treaty for European Union and the intergovernmental Dooge Committee Report, came to the conclusion that the existing Treaty of Rome needed amending. Mrs. Thatcher opposed this view so vigorously that, contrary to past practice in European Council meetings, the issue was put to a vote by the Italian Prime Minister. A clear majority voted in favour of a conference to negotiate a new treaty. Britain fell into line and Mrs. Thatcher took full part in the negotiations which led to the signing and the subsequent parliamentary ratification of the Single European Act.

Suppose that Britain were faced with a stark choice of either going along with her Community partners towards full monetary, economic, and political union, or being left behind, whilst the others were ready to go ahead on their own. It is inconceivable that a responsible British government would repeat and pay the heavy price for failing to join the Community at its inception. Excluded for fifteen years, Britain's economy fell behind and her influence in world affairs declined dramatically. The cost of that isolation, still fresh in the minds of Britain's politicians and senior civil servants, is one that they would not be willing to pay again. Most of Mrs. Thatcher's cabinet colleagues and leading members of the Conservative Party, senior civil servants, as well as commerce and industry did not countenance Britain being relegated to second-class status and becoming isolated in Europe once again. On this key issue of Britain's future destiny Mrs. Thatcher was forced to resign her premiership.

Chapter two

The emerging union

The dramatic changes in the nature of the world, which have taken place since the Second World War, have had a particularly profound impact upon relations between states in Europe. Nationalism and demands for democratic self-determination, increasingly articulated after the popular uprising throughout central Europe in 1848, finally found satisfaction with the collapse of the German, Austro-Hungarian, Russian, and Ottoman empires as a result of the First World War. President Woodrow Wilson's Fourteen Points, the Versailles Treaty and the Covenant of the League of Nations of 1919 were all concerned with establishing independent and sovereign nation states in their place. It was a proud boast that the new national political frontiers, established by the Treaty, were so drawn that only 3 per cent of the European continent's total population lived under alien rule. Judged by the test of democratic national self-determination, no previous European frontiers had been so satisfactory.

Yet, over the following twenty years, democracy in many European countries gave way to totalitarian regimes sustained by aggressive economic and political nationalism. The League of Nations, meant to regulate relations between sovereign states, lacked effective powers to impose its collective will. It weakened and finally collapsed in the face of fascist and nazi aggression. The advent of the Second World War finally persuaded European countries to seek a new settlement, which would secure peace and move beyond the classic league of independent states towards a very much more far-reaching economic and political union.

Central to post-war development in western Europe has been the contribution of federal ideas. Indeed, the whole history of European integration has been dominated by an intensive debate between protagonists of federal solutions and those defending increasingly out-dated notions of national sovereignty. It has also been a debate between pragmatists, who believe that the best way to proceed is to react to events in a practical way, without necessarily defining or even knowing their ultimate aim, and the so-called visionaries who believe that all action should be guided by progress towards a clear objective. This chapter gives account of the debate and the resulting developments.

Unity by consent

European history recounts several attempts to unite the continent under single rule. In the first and second centuries AD the Roman Empire included all the territories in North Africa, Asia Minor and Europe bordering on the Mediterranean Sea, and the rest of colonized Europe stretching from Britain to the Black Sea. Emperor Charlemagne ruled in 800 AD over most of western Christendom. In the sixteenth century, through marriage and by force of arms, the Holy Roman Emperor Charles V controlled Europe from Gibraltar to Hungary and from Amsterdam to Sicily. In 1810 Napoleon's empire extended from Spain to the borders of the Russian and Ottoman empires. Finally Hitler by 1942, in pursuit of his goal of a Greater Germany that would last a thousand years, conquered territory in Europe extending from the Pyrenees to the outskirts of Leningrad, Moscow and Stalingrad, and from Norway to Greece. Yet, apart from the Roman Empire, none of the others endured for long and most of them did not survive their architects.

Our story, however, is concerned with uniting our continent by consent of its citizens instead of by conquest – an attempt that, because of this vital difference, offers the near certainty that it will endure. Serious considerations to unite started this century. A seminal book *The Great Illusion* by Norman Angell, first published in 1908, analysed the rivalries between the great powers and causes of war between them. Translated into many languages, continuously reprinted with occasional new editions over the following thirty years, it influenced many who were seeking a different way of conducting international relations. The nub of his argument, appearing in one of the later editions, was contained in the following passage (Angell 1933):

If, in what is now the United States, there had developed from the original thirteen colonies half-a-dozen independent sovereign nations (as the Spanish American colonies developed into a dozen nations) each with its own army, navy, tariff, currency, they would have fought each other as Bolivia fights Paraguay, Chile and Peru. If Pennsylvania does *not* fight Ohio, but France does fight Germany, it is not because those who live in Pittsburgh or Toledo are necessarily superior in social morality or intention, or in peacefulness, to those living in Cologne or Lille, but because history has developed a federal bond in the one case, and not in the other. If, by some happy accident of European history some form of federal bond had been left (as a legacy, say, of the Roman Empire) so that we had to-day a United States of Europe in which France and Germany occupied much the position that Pennsylvania and Ohio occupy in the American system – or if they occupied the position of a French or German Canton in the Swiss Confederation – war would have been as unknown between the two Rhine nations, as it is between States of the American Union.

With the approach of the First World War many attempts were made to promote peace through federal means. Albert Einstein, Lujo Brentano, Prince Lichnovsky, and others set up Neues Vaterland in Berlin in 1914. Article 1 of its objects was: 'the promotion of all efforts to imbue the policy of the European powers with civilised notions of peaceful competition and supranational unification'. The Union of Democratic Control founded in London in 1914 by Ramsay MacDonald, Charles Trevelyan, and Norman Angell issued a Manifesto urging that 'policy should no longer be arrived at through a balance of power but should be directed to establishing a European Federation of States'. A Dutch committee set up in the same year called for Europe to become 'a closely united league of states or a federal state'. Although their voices were not heeded and Europe plunged into the First World War that claimed millions of lives, the ideas were not dead. Walther Rathenau, in 1918, later to be assassinated after he became German Foreign Minister, called for the replacement of 'international anarchy by a voluntarily accepted higher authority' (Lipgens 1986).

League of Nations

The Versailles Peace Conference in 1919 chose, however, a different path. The League of Nations, established by the Treaty of Versailles, was created to promote international co-operation and to achieve international peace and security. Membership was not, however, compulsory and the USA never joined it. Germany became a permanent member in 1926 but resigned in 1933 after Hitler came to power. Japan, after being condemned for aggression in China, also resigned in 1933. Italy followed in 1937 after successfully defying the League over her conquest of Abyssinia, a country that was also a member of the League. The failure of the League of Nations to maintain international peace was largely due to national sovereignty remaining unfettered and from the lack of effective sanctions to secure compliance with League decisions. The existence of the League did, however, for a time, put European unification on the back burner.

In 1923, in a book entitled *Paneuropa*, Austrian Count Coudenhove-Kalergi argued that the unification of the nations of Europe 'will either come voluntarily through the formation of a European federation or will be forced on Europe by a Russian conquest' (Coudenhove-Kalergi 1966). He founded the Pan-Europa Union which quickly gained a large membership and much public support. At its first congress in Vienna in October 1926 over 2,000 European politicians, educationalists, businessmen, lawyers, and journalists demanded the 'political and economic unification of all states from Portugal to Poland' and the progressive development of 'a United States of Europe'.

Elected President of the Pan-Europa Union in 1927, French Foreign Minister Aristide Briand, decided to take a major initiative in pursuit of the Union's objective. Addressing the Assembly of the League of Nations in September 1929, Briand proposed a project for the establishment of a European federal union. His detailed Memorandum *On the organisation of a Europe Federal Union* was sent to all European governments in May 1930. The responses received showed, however, a complete miscomprehension, especially by those larger powers, for whom the ceding of national sovereignty was inconceivable. Indeed the emerging world economic crisis of the 1930s stimulated defensive measures of national protection and a growing authoritarianism that, like fascism and national socialism, proclaimed the nation state as the sole arbiter of its destiny. Aggressive designs upon weaker neighbours threatened the international order and made war increasingly likely.

The federal alternative

In a public lecture in 1935 Philip Kerr, later to become Lord Lothian, declared that 'war is inherent in an international system based on national sovereignty'. A growing body of intellectuals backed federalism as a solution to the problems of war. In Britain they included Norman Angell, H.N. Brailsford, G.D.H. Cole, Harold Laski, R.H. Tawney, and Leonard Woolf. Lionel Robbins, at the beginning of 1939, applied a federalist analysis to the international economic crisis in a series of prestigious lectures delivered in Geneva, which were later published as *The Economic Causes of War* (Robbins 1939).

Indeed, London became the centre from which the federal idea received a new lease of life. In 1938 a number of young men, deeply concerned at the seemingly inevitable progress towards war, decided to launch a movement in favour of a democratic European organization with supranational powers that became known as Federal Union (Mayne, *et al.* forthcoming). They appealed to several hundred selected personalities in public life for support. Some thirty-five prominent people, including Lionel Curtis, Lord Lothian, Lionel Robbins, Arnold Toynbee, former *Times* editor Henry Wickham Steed, J.B. Priestley, Ralph Vaughan Williams, and Barbara Wootton, signed a declaration 'that national sovereignty had to be overcome and that federation must replace it'.

Widely publicized, the declaration gained Federal Union several thousand supporters. At its first national conference of local groups and branches, held in July 1939, it set up a National Council. Considerable interest in the federal idea was stimulated by two influential books published in London at the time. They were *Union Now* by the American Clarence Streit and *The Case for Federal Union* by W.B. Curry. But the movement was too late to avert the war.

After the outbreak of the war considerable thought was given to the development and publication of a series of closely argued tracts on federal themes. Sir William Beveridge, Master of University College, Oxford, chaired the newly established Federal Union Research Institute. A major intellectual input came from people like Professor Ivor Jennings, Lionel Curtis, Kenneth Wheare, Lionel Robbins, James Meade, Friedrich von Hayek, Harold Wilson, Barbara Wootton, and others.

Anglo-French Union

In the autumn of 1939 the concept of a European Federation based on Britain and France, to be joined after the war by a democratic Germany, gained in strength. The Foreign Office worked on a scheme for an Anglo-French Union, a project which secured Prime Minister Neville Chamberlain's backing on 1 March 1940. Arnold Toynbee, then at Chatham House, drew up, on the basis of the Foreign Office project, an Act of Perpetual Association between France and Britain which was approved by the Foreign Secretary Lord Halifax and by Sir Alexander Cadogan, his permanent secretary.

In the meantime German troops, after invading Holland and Belgium, advanced into France, where resistance started to crumble. To stop the final collapse, Jean Monnet, an Anglo-French civil servant co-ordinating Allied war supplies, decided to seize the initiative (Monnet 1976). He proposed a dramatic declaration by the two governments of the solidarity of British and French interests through the merger of their respective governments into a single cabinet and by uniting their two parliaments. His ideas gained support from some British civil servants and from General de Gaulle. Neville Chamberlain persuaded Winston Churchill, his successor as Premier, to include the project on the cabinet agenda. To the latter's surprise it received enthusiastic support amongst his colleagues. As a result on 16 June the Cabinet agreed to propose to the French Government that 'France and Britain shall no longer be two nations but one Franco-British Union'.

Paul Reynaud, the French Prime Minister to whom de Gaulle had transmitted the text of the British declaration, recognized that the proposal could avert the collapse of French resistance and argued forcefully its acceptance by his own cabinet colleagues. French defeatism had however reached a point of no return. His pleas fell mostly on deaf ears and by the next day he was forced to resign. Marshall Pétain took his place determined to seek an armistice.

Planning for peace

Although Monnet's initiative failed on this occasion, detailed discussions continued about a post-war organization of Europe on federal lines. Governments of occupied countries, exiled to Britain, were much involved. An international committee of Federal Union, which included representatives of sixteen European countries, was formed in 1941. By July 1943 they produced two memoranda advocating a European federation.

East European representatives were particularly strongly in favour of union. In 1941 Polish, Czech, Yugoslav, and Greek representatives negotiated a Declaration of Solidarity between their governments. General Sikorski, leader of the Polish government in London, favoured the unification of the whole of Europe with a federal union between Poland and Czechoslovakia as a first step. He persuaded President Beneš to sign a Czechoslovak-Polish confederal treaty in January 1942. Amongst the west Europeans, Belgian Foreign Minister Paul-Henri Spaak negotiated with his Netherlands and Luxembourg colleagues and by 1944 they agreed to set up the Benelux Customs Union.

Reflecting these discussions and his own growing commitment to some permanent organization of post-war Europe, Winston Churchill wrote the following on 21 October 1942 in a minute to his Foreign Secretary: 'Hard as it is to say now, I trust that the European family may act unitedly as one under a Council of Europe. I look forward to a United States of Europe in which the barriers between the nations will be greatly minimised and unrestricted travel will be possible. I hope to see the economy of Europe studied as a whole.'

On 21 March 1943, in a broadcast beamed worldwide, Churchill called for the establishment after the war of a Council of Europe in which both victor and vanquished would participate. As he put it:

We must try to make the Council of Europe, or whatever it may be called, into a really effective League, with all the strongest forces concerned woven into its texture, with a High Court to adjust disputes, with forces, armed force, national or international or both, held ready to enforce the decisions and prevent renewed aggression and the preparation of future wars.

The Federal Union tracts and the recommendations of the exiled governments were smuggled into occupied Europe and distributed amongst resistance movements. Many of the latter developed the ideas further in planning for the post-war world. Some books and pamphlets by the British federalists reached Mussolini's political prisoners confined on the island of Ventotene off Naples. Altiero Spinelli and Ernesto Rossi, two of their leaders, after intensive study of the literature received, issued the Ventotene Manifesto in 1941 which provided the intellectual foundation of the Italian Federalist Movement launched in August 1943. After the liberation, Spinelli and Rossi went to Geneva to organize a meeting of representatives of resistance groups from several countries to work out a common programme. The final Declaration of the conference calling for a European Federation owed much to the ideas worked out by Federal Union.

In the meantime, Jean Monnet, by now with the Free French in Algiers, was also engaged in planning for peace. He wrote:

There will be no peace in Europe if States reconstitute themselves on a basis of national sovereignty . . . European countries are too confined to ensure prosperity and essential social developments for their people. It follows that European States should form themselves into a federation or a 'European entity' which would make them a joint economic unit.

As the liberation of the Continent progressed, federalist organizations sprang up in various countries. A conference on European Federation was held in Paris in March 1945. It was opened by the French author Albert Camus followed by Spinelli and attended by federalists from France, Italy, Switzerland, Austria, Germany, Spain, Greece, and Britain, including George Orwell. Dutch, Belgian, and German branches of Federal Union were formed soon after. At international meetings held in 1946 at Hertenstein, near Lucerne in Switzerland, in Luxembourg and in Paris it was agreed to found the European Union of Federalists which was to play a central part in the battle for European unification.

Meanwhile Churchill, after his defeat in the 1945 General Election, decided to absent himself from Parliament for a few months and undertake a series of speaking engagements in America and Europe about the state of the world and his vision for the future. In March 1946 he delivered a speech in Fulton, Missouri, in which he first spoke publicly about the division of Europe. As he put it: 'From Stettin in the Baltic to Trieste in the Adriatic, an iron curtain has descended across the Continent.' Whilst he did not regard war with Russia as imminent or inevitable, he argued for a policy of strength and unity in the face of the Soviet Union and its central and eastern European communist satellites.

Speaking in western Europe, Churchill developed his ideas about European unity. In November 1945 in Brussels, he first mentioned the idea of 'the United States of Europe'. In September 1946 he delivered a speech in Zurich that caught the imagination throughout Europe. In it he spoke of the post-war distress for which he saw, as a remedy, a partnership between France and Germany and the building of 'a kind of United States of Europe'. It was remarkable that so soon after the end of the war he recognized the crucial importance of Franco-German reconciliation. Although during the war he appeared to link Britain fully with the future of Europe, he now appeared more ambivalent about it. To him the British Empire and Commonwealth came first and the relationship with Europe only in some form of close but external association.

Economic crisis

At the time, Europe faced the dislocation of the entire fabric of its economy. Machinery was obsolete or in disrepair, currencies were discredited, and, as people despaired, social unrest grew. At the end of the war American Lend-Lease was stopped abruptly. Loans raised in the USA by individual European countries, intended for investment and future reconstruction, were having to be spent on raw materials and the immediate consumption of food and fuel.

The Americans came to realize that if Europe's economy collapsed the US would suffer gravely and that for the sake of political stability and economic health the Americans had to act. In June 1947 General Marshall, the American Secretary of State, offered to provide essential financial and economic help for European recovery. His offer was conditional on the Europeans co-ordinating their needs and acting together in allocating the aid. The west Europeans responded with alacrity; but, although the offer was extended to the whole of Europe, the Russians refused the Marshall offer. They dubbed it a programme to interfere in the internal affairs of other states. Eastern European countries under Soviet control were instructed to reject the offer too. And so the Marshall Plan, without the involvement of communist controlled Europe, laid the foundation for economic co-operation between democratic states alone. By April 1948, under American pressure, the recipients of the aid agreed to set up the Organization for European Economic Co-operation that took responsibility for co-ordinating the American aid and liberating intra-European trade.

Following the Soviet rejection of the Marshall Plan, the cold war in

Europe grew. In February 1948 a Communist coup took place in Czechoslovakia and a month later Jan Masaryk, Czech Foreign Minister since 1940, son of the country's first President and a strong protagonist of European unity, took his life or, as some suspect, was murdered. In response to the growing threat from the east, the governments of Britain, France, Belgium, The Netherlands, and Luxembourg signed a treaty in Brussels establishing a joint defence pact. They did not, however, possess adequate forces on their own and immediately approached the US Government for American involvement. Within eleven months an alliance with the USA and Canada was negotiated and the North Atlantic Treaty Organization (NATO) was established.

Congress of Europe

All these events added urgency to the attempts to move from rhetoric to action in uniting Europe. At the initiative of Churchill's son-in-law, Duncan Sandys, the various organizations working for European unity were brought together at the first Congress of Europe in May 1948 in The Hague. Some 750 people, representing almost every European nationality, attended as delegates. There were also observers from the USA and the British Commonwealth and 250 or so members of the world's press. Over fifty of the delegates were former Prime Ministers, Foreign Ministers and serving cabinet ministers. Churchill presided as Chairman of the Congress. The political committee was presided over by former French Socialist Prime Minister, Paul Ramadier, the economic committee by former Belgian Premier, Paul Van Zeeland, and the cultural committee by the distinguished Spanish author, Professor Salvador de Madariaga.

Final resolutions of the Congress formed the basis of pressure soon to be exerted on European governments by the principal congress delegates. The political resolution called for a European Union or Federation to which individual nations would transfer some of their sovereign rights, so as to act politically and economically together and aim at integrating and developing their common resources. Germany would form part of it. A European Assembly, chosen by the Parliaments of the participating nations, was to be urgently convened to advise on the measures needed to achieve the political and economic union of Europe. Membership would be open to all European democracies willing to subscribe to a Charter of Human Rights. A Court of Justice with powers to implement the Charter was to be set up. The economic resolution called for the free movement of people, goods, and capital, a customs union and monetary unification. In the cultural field recommendations included the setting up of a European Cultural Centre and the promotion of European education.

Finally, to further the aims of the Congress, it was agreed to found the European Movement as an independent pressure group, with Duncan Sandys as its first international President. Forty years after its formation the Movement continues to play the co-ordinating role in fourteen European countries for all voluntary organizations working for European unity.

Council of Europe

Several political and institutional developments stemmed from the recommendations of the Congress. There was the European Payments Union, the European Cultural Foundation in Amsterdam, and the College of Europe in Bruges. But by far the most significant development was an agreement to set up a Consultative Assembly of members of national parliaments and a Committee of Ministers to be known as the Council of Europe. The Statute of the Council of Europe was signed in London on 5 May 1949 – a date which was fixed as the official Europe Day. The signatories were the five Brussels Pact members together with Denmark, Norway, Sweden, Ireland, and Italy. Its declared aim was to achieve a closer union between its members in economic, social, scientific, legal, and administrative matters. It further concerned itself with the promotion and protection of human rights and fundamental liberties. It adopted the European Convention for the Protection of Human Rights and set up the European Court whose judgements were to be binding on member states.

At its first meeting in August 1949 the Assembly elected former Belgian Premier and Foreign Minister Paul-Henri Spaak as its President. At the end of the first session he declared: 'I came to Strasbourg convinced of the need for a United States of Europe. I leave with the certainty that union is possible.' The Council of Europe was the first European political organization. Its Assembly members, appointed by national parliaments, sat in the Chamber by alphabetical order and not in national delegations, and voted as individuals. Yet it became a place of disappointed hopes. It never acquired legislative powers. The Committee of Ministers could only make recommendations to member governments and these in practice required unanimous agreement, so that there could be no agreement if any one minister objected. It is therefore hardly surprising that the Council was unable to fulfil the hopes of The Hague Congress for a political union. Within two years of taking office, Spaak resigned disillusioned. As he put it later: 'of all the international bodies I have known, I have never found any more timorous or more impotent'.

Integration on federal lines

Meanwhile, world events gave ever more urgency to the need for European unity. The Berlin blockade by the Russians started in August 1948. A year later the Soviet Union admitted that it possessed the atomic bomb. At about the same time the newly elected German Chancellor, Konrad Adenauer, announced that the Federal Republic wished to join not only the Council of Europe but also the Atlantic Alliance. German industrial reconstruction was also making remarkable progress. French alarm at the re-establishment of a major industrial and possibly military power on its borders, urgently concentrated the minds of French leaders. Jean Monnet saw his opportunity to subsume the German problem. He submitted to the French Government a proposal 'to place the whole of Franco-German coal and steel production under a common High Authority, in an organization open to the participation of the other countries of Europe'. Whilst Germany would once again be treated as an equal, the pooling of basic resources would make war between France and Germany 'not only unthinkable but materially impossible'.

The French Government approved the plan and Foreign Minister Robert Schuman, in a declaration made public on 9 May 1950, proposed the creation of the European Coal and Steel Community (ECSC) to establish a common basis for economic development and as a first step to the federation of Europe. The common High Authority would become a European power independent of the member states in the fields entrusted to it. Schuman made this principle of supranationality a prior condition for negotiations on a treaty to set up the Community. Six countries declared their acceptance of the proposal, namely France, Germany, Italy, and three Benelux countries. Britain's Labour Government, which had only recently and with difficulty nationalized its coal and steel industries, was unwilling to cede control of them to a supranational organization and declined the invitation.

The Treaty of Paris, setting up the ECSC was signed on 18 April 1951. In addition to the independent supranational High Authority, the Treaty provided for a Common Assembly, composed of national parliamentarians, to exercise democratic control over the executive, and a Court of Justice to resolve disputes and whose decisions were binding on the members. The recommendations of the High Authority had to be approved by a special Council of Ministers representing the member states. Some of their decisions, according to the treaty, were taken by qualified majority, others by unanimous agreement.

Now the question arose of how to move from a sectoral authority to a genuine political power with much wider jurisdiction. Proposals were soon made for supranational authorities in other fields such as transport, public health, and agriculture, but these did not receive much support from member governments.

Defence

Added urgency for further European integration came following the outbreak of the Korean war in June 1950. The North Koreans, fully armed and backed by the Russians, seemed to provide a dress rehearsal for what might soon happen in Europe. Soviet troops and those of its satellites heavily outnumbered allied forces in Europe. The Americans were fighting in Korea, the French in Indo-China and British troops were scattered all over the world. Only Germany could make a significant contribution to common defence. Yet the re-armament of Germany was very difficult for the French to swallow. Jean Monnet urged once again 'to integrate Germany into Europe by means of a broader Schuman Plan, taking the necessary decisions within a European framework'. He persuaded the new French Premier, René Pleven, to present his plan to the French National Assembly. He proposed 'the creation, for common defence, of a European Army under the authority of the political institutions of a united Europe'. The Assembly approved the plan and for a brief period it seemed that a United States of Europe would be achieved.

Negotiations started in February 1951 with all European members of NATO invited to participate. Whilst Britain, hostile to federalist objectives, once again refused to take part, a Treaty establishing a European Defence Community was negotiated and signed between the six ECSC members in May 1952. Yet the creation of the EDC posed the problem of adequate democratic and political control. It was realized that a political authority was an essential accompaniment to a European army. A special article was therefore included in the EDC Treaty for a democratic assembly to exercise such control. The Assembly of the Coal and Steel Community was to be entrusted with drafting a Treaty constituting a European Political Authority.

By 1954, however, difficulties arose over the ratification of the Defence Community Treaty. After the fall of several French governments and Britain's refusal to join the EDC, circumstances were changing. The death of Stalin promised a possible lessening of the cold war and the need to build a European army became less urgent. Although France had been the strongest protagonist of supranational institutions, the new French Government of Pierre Mendès-France was lukewarm. Opponents of federal solutions and protagonists of French independence and national sovereignty were gaining the upper hand. In August 1954 Mendès-France presented the EDC Treaty for ratification in a non-committal speech and the French National Assembly failed to approve it. Thus the EDC was killed, as was the proposal for a European Political Community. As one consequence, Germany soon became a full member of the Atlantic Alliance.

After the collapse of the EDC there was fear amongst supporters of European unification that the partially supranational ECSC might also be swept away. European leaders such as Spaak, Monnet, Adenauer, and the Dutch Foreign Minister, Johan Beyen, feared that time was against them unless unification was given a new impulse. Two factors were clear. There was no chance of creating a federal state in the immediate future. It was, however, becoming increasingly obvious that no individual west European state would on its own be able to solve its economic problems.

Economic Community

Monnet favoured another sectoral step forward. He wanted nuclear power and its development for peaceful purposes to be added to the responsibilities of the Coal and Steel Community. The Benelux countries and the Germans on the other hand favoured the creation of a customs union. To persuade the French to take part in discussions on wider economic issues, the others decided to support Monnet's proposals on atomic energy. A conference of foreign ministers was convened at Messina in June 1955. At the end of difficult negotiations agreement was reached to create two new organizations, one an atomic community and another for a common market. Spaak, with a small group of experts, was entrusted with drawing up a plan of action. His report, delivered in 1956, became the guiding document for the intergovernmental negotiations that started in June of that year.

The failure of the Anglo-French Suez adventure had a traumatic effect on the French. They realized that their days as a world power were over. And so when discussions were held in the French National Assembly in January 1957, general approval was voiced in favour of closer co-operation with the other European states, Indeed the weak economic position of the country left them little alternative but to go along with proposals to join an economic community. By February negotiations were completed. France was to enter the common market together with her overseas dependencies and the ownership of fissile materials was to be vested in Euratom. The Treaties were signed in Rome on 25 March 1957.

The EEC Treaty was separate from that of the Coal and Steel Community but the institutional framework was similar, with a Council of Ministers retaining ultimate control over decisions and legislation, and a Commission acting as the executive organ guiding the Community towards its Treaty objectives. A Court of Justice would adjudicate and a parliamentary Assembly, in due course to be directly elected, would have a largely consultative role. The Treaty thus contained both intergovernmental and supranational elements. Some decisions were subject to qualified majority voting, others, particularly in adopting new responsibilities or policies, required unanimous agreement. Progress towards full federation was not spelt out but neither was it excluded. It all depended on the political will of member states.

Invited, Britain sent a civil servant as an observer to the Messina conference, but it did not accept the Messina resolution. When the negotiations progressed towards the creation of a customs union, Britain decided to withdraw, doubting whether, as in the case of the EDC, anything would come of them. When the Treaty was actually signed and soon afterwards ratified by all of its six members, alarm bells started ringing in Westminster. If the Common Market of the Six was becoming a reality, Britain faced economic isolation from the Continent and had to rethink its strategy. Britain proposed an industrial free trade area that excluded agriculture. To strengthen her bargaining power Britain formed the European Free Trade Area, with six other European countries that did not belong to the EEC, with the object of merging EFTA and the EEC into a wider free trade area. The proposal was, however, doomed from the start because it ignored the commitment of the Six to the Economic Community, including agriculture, which they conceived as another major step towards further political integration. Britain's approach was rebuffed because the Six, and France in particular, were not prepared to water down their existing arrangements or abandon ultimate union.

Gaullist break on progress

When General de Gaulle came to power in France in 1958, progress towards the federation of Europe faced a new obstacle. Although de Gaulle was in favour of closer European political co-operation, he was critical of the EC method with its supranational elements. These he wanted to subordinate to intergovernmental political control. He was hostile to the ECSC and EURATOM and was showing concern about the growing authority of the EC Commission. He opposed direct elections to the parliamentary Assembly and wanted the existing Communities capped with an interstate political organization in which individual national sovereignty would be preserved by the unanimity rule. Whilst France's partners were ready to talk about political co-operation in fields not covered by the existing Communities, none of them was willing to give up the supranational elements.

Following a conference of the six Heads of State in Paris early in

1961, a preparatory working committee was set up under a French chairman Christian Fouchet. During the same year Britain applied for full membership of the EC. The Benelux governments and Italy were willing to discuss political co-operation, provided that nothing would affect the status of NATO or the British desire to join the Community. As the subsequent negotiations were to show, there was no ultimate meeting of minds. De Gaulle wanted a 'Europe of the States' with no supranationality in politics or economics and a European Europe with its own distinctive foreign and defence policy guided by France. The others, and in particular the Dutch, wanted full economic integration and no political union without Britain, which was seen as the guarantor of Europe's commitment to the Atlantic Alliance. As a result the various proposals from the Fouchet Committee failed, and political union disappeared from the European agenda throughout the remainder of General de Gaulle's Presidency of France.

Indeed de Gaulle's reaction showed a growing hostility to the European Community and its further enlargement and development. When Britain was rebuffed over her proposal for a wider free trade area, the British Premier Harold Macmillan decided to seek full membership of the EC in 1961. Ireland, Denmark, and Norway applied alongside. The British negotiations were conducted by Edward Heath and seemed close to success when in January 1963 de Gaulle used the occasion of Macmillan's decision to acquire the American Polaris missiles to declare a French veto on British entry.

Although initially there was bad feeling about the veto amongst France's partners, the Community continued to develop, with major decisions being taken on the common agricultural policy. Yet there was a growing divergence between the federalist and Gaullist positions. On 1 January 1966 the major exceptions to the use of majority voting, allowed during the first eight transitional years of the Treaty, were to come to an end, so that theoretically an individual country could be outvoted. The completion of the industrial customs union and the agricultural common market were planned for mid-1967. A single external tariff and agreement to transfer income from agricultural levies to the Community was the starting point for a federal budget. The Dutch would not agree to this unless the budget became subject to more effective democratic accountability by strengthening the budgetary powers of the European Parliament. In response to this view the European Commission submitted a package proposal for direct revenues for the Community and for an effective budgetary vote for the European Parliament.

The French wanted the proposed financial regulation, which would pay for the agricultural policy, but refused any increase in the Parliament's powers. At the Council of Ministers in June 1965 no agreement was reached and France decided to boycott the Community's decision-making mechanism, in direct breach of her Treaty obligations. The other five continued to meet while the French chair remained empty. In September de Gaulle called for a revision of the treaties. He refused to accept majority voting that was due to come into force in 1966, as it would deprive France of her sovereignty. The five were not prepared to yield. Indeed, as majority voting was to come in on 1 January, subsequent French absence would not stop the others from taking decisions on their own.

Pressures in France, however, began to tell. The farmers and industrial and financial circles feared the economic consequences of the boycott, let alone a break with the Community. In the December 1965 French presidential elections the candidate of the centre, Jean Lecanuet, and that of the socialists, François Mitterrand, strongly criticized the French Government's position. Indeed Lecanuet called for rapid progress towards a federal political union with direct elections to the European Parliament. His unexpectedly high vote of 17 per cent forced de Gaulle into a second round in which he faced Mitterrand who also took a strong pro-European stance, echoing Lecanuet's demand for a directly elected European Parliament.

The attack on the Community was clearly unpopular and the government decided to cut its losses and return to the Community's negotiating table on the best possible terms. The basic French demand presented at the Council meeting in Luxembourg early in 1966 was that majority voting was not to be used where a 'vital national interest' was at stake. As each state would be free to define its own vital national interest, the effect would be that the Community would abandon its supranational features and all decisions would be subject to unanimous agreement. The other five refused to accept this change. In the end they agreed that, where very important national interests were at stake for one or more countries, every attempt should be made to achieve unanimity. The French wanted to add that negotiations should continue until unanimity was reached, but the five others disagreed. The so-called Luxembourg compromise was in effect an agreement to disagree. The Treaty was left intact, but in practice no major decisions were taken without unanimous agreement.

There followed a period of relative stagnation. The dismantling of customs barriers and the liberalization of internal trade in industrial goods continued – indeed the customs union was achieved in July 1968, eighteen months ahead of schedule – but no new policies emerged. Although the timetables were adhered to, the Community marked time over further integration or development. Britain's second attempt to join in 1967 was vetoed by de Gaulle within six months of the application. It became increasingly clear that as long as de Gaulle remained at the head of the French Government further progress within the Community would be blocked.

End of stagnation and enlargement

The break came with de Gaulle's resignation in April 1969, following the defeat of his proposals for regional devolution in France and which had been submitted to a national referendum. At The Hague Summit meeting in December 1969 French President Pompidou, who succeeded de Gaulle, negotiated financial arrangements for the agricultural policy which replaced national contributions with the Community's own financial resources. It was, furthermore, agreed to open negotiations for British entry. The meeting also considered ways in which progress could be made to full Economic and Monetary Union, and the task was entrusted to an ad hoc group, chaired by Luxembourg's Prime Minister, Pierre Werner. The Foreign Ministers were also instructed to submit proposals for political unification by the following July. The final declaration of the Summit, announcing that 'The Community has today arrived at a turning point in its history', clearly marked the resumption of progress.

Following the Summit, negotiations settled the system of the Community's own financial resources, through the payment to the Community of all agricultural levies and customs duties and up to 1 per cent of the receipts from value added tax. This decision was accompanied by a new Treaty of Luxembourg which in part transferred national parliamentary control of national contributions to the European Parliament by strengthening its budgetary powers.

Negotiations for the admission of Britain, Ireland, Denmark and Norway started in June 1970 and were successfully concluded by the Summer of 1971. The British House of Commons approved the terms of membership by a majority of 112, aided by the fact that sixty-nine Labour MPs defied their party and joined most of the Conservatives in voting in favour.

In Denmark and Ireland there were large referenda majorities in favour. Only in Norway was membership rejected by a narrow referendum majority. After parliamentary ratification by the applicant countries and the Six, Britain, Denmark and Ireland joined the Community in January 1973.

Economic and Monetary Union

In the meantime consideration was given to the Werner Report on Economic and Monetary Union (EC Commission 1970). The report recommended a decision-making centre for monetary policy, a

Community system of central banks, and supervision by the European Parliament. Integration would proceed by stages, in the first of which monetary fluctuations between Community currencies were to be limited through co-ordinated interventions. The Council of Ministers, meeting in February 1971, did not accept the institutional proposals though it did agree to increase co-ordination of economic policies between members, strengthen co-operation between central banks, and establish methods for providing medium-term financial help. In the monetary field it was agreed that the maximum permitted fluctuation margins between members' currencies would be limited to 2.25 per cent.

This last proposal was popularly known as the 'snake in the tunnel', the tunnel being the agreement to reduce fluctuations against the US Dollar to 4.5 per cent. The snake was finally agreed by the Central banks in April 1974, but it soon collapsed. Following the oil crisis and the massive rise in the cost of primary products, major monetary instability and inflation threatened the agreements reached. By the middle of 1974 Britain, France and Ireland had left the snake, and pressures on the economies of the other member states soon rendered all progress towards the Werner Report version of monetary and economic union politically no longer practicable.

Towards Union

Much better progress was, however, achieved in the field of political co-operation, called for by the 1969 Summit. Foreign Ministers were instructed to 'study the best way of achieving progress in the matter of political unification, within the context of enlargement'. After relatively speedy negotiations, Community Foreign Ministers adopted, in October 1970, the Davignon Report prepared by the political director of the Belgian Foreign Ministry (EC Commission 1970). The essence of his report was that harmonization of foreign policy was the first step towards political union. Its recommendations were that intergovernmental co-operation should start outside the Community framework, through regular exchange of information between foreign ministries, aimed at promoting the harmonization of views and, where possible, instigating common action. Over the years that followed, voluntary political co-operation was strengthened through the adoption of common positions and the co-ordination of diplomatic action in all international affairs affecting the interests of the European Community. Proposals to establish a permanent secretariat for political co-operation were not, however, accepted because some members were not prepared to see an institutional development outside the framework of the European Community.

Successful progress towards enlargement, economic and monetary union and political co-operation had, by the autumn of 1972, persuaded the Heads of Governments, meeting in Paris, to chart an even more ambitious programme, accompanied by a series of deadlines. These included setting up a European Monetary Co-operation Fund to prepare for full Economic and Monetary Union by 1980. A Regional Development Fund was to be established, as well as a series of action programmes for the protection of the environment, social policy, and science and technology. In conclusion the Heads of Governments declared their intention 'to transform the whole complex of their relations into a European Union by the end of the present decade'. To ensure progress towards it, the leaders asked the Community institutions to draw up a report on the issue before the end of 1975 for submission to another summit conference.

The failure of the Economic and Monetary Union after the world oil crisis persuaded Community governments to make a new attempt to revive progress towards unity. At the Paris Summit of December 1974 three significant decisions were taken. First, to proceed to direct elections of the European Parliament, then to institutionalize summit meetings by creating the European Council of Heads of Governments, meeting three times a year, and finally, they asked the Belgian Prime Minister, Leo Tindemans, to draw up a report on the concept and shape of European Union (EC Commission 1976). The importance of these decisions lay in the democratization of the Community and the creation of the European Council to determine the direction of Community development and resolve conflicts that impeded progress.

The Tindemans Report, submitted in January 1976, took account of the generally lukewarm climate towards major change amongst member governments at a stage when they were facing a continuing world economic crisis. It identified the main aspects of the proposed union as presenting a united front to the outside world. It recognized that economic interdependence of members states required common policies, which included regional and social responsibilities, to ensure solidarity between them. It called for the development of a greater public awareness of Europe and the enhancement of the authority, effectiveness, and legitimacy of the Community's institutions. It did not, however, lay down any detailed plan to be carried out in stages, as did the original Spaak Report that led to the setting up of the EEC and Euratom. It was hardly surprising, therefore, that the Report had very little effect on the decisions of member governments. The only practical outcome was an invitation to the Council and the Commission to submit annual reports on progress towards the vaguely defined European Union.

The grand design to achieve European Union by 1980 came to

nothing. There were only two significant developments that took place before the end of the decade. One was the agreement at the December 1975 Summit to organize the first direct elections to the European Parliament in 1978. By September 1976 agreement on the composition of the Parliament and details of the electoral law were adopted by the Council of Ministers. Owing to delays in the ratification of the electoral law by the national parliaments, the elections had to be postponed to June 1979. The powers of the elected Parliament remained unchanged from those of its nominated predecessor. Apart from its power to approve the Community budget, its only sanction lay in the right to censure the Commission. Its legislative functions were largely consultative. It was clear that the battle for more powers lay ahead.

European Monetary System

The other development arose from a desire to find another way towards economic and monetary unification, following the failure of the Werner Plan. The European monetary snake had lost most of its original participants and by 1979 only five members remained part of it, namely Germany, Denmark, and the Benelux countries. In his Monnet Lecture in Florence, in October 1977, the President of the European Commission, Roy Jenkins, proposed the establishment of a new monetary system. The object was to create a zone of monetary stability in the Community and establish closer financial co-operation. During the subsequent negotiations, spread over four Summits from April 1978 to March 1979, comprehensive agreement was negotiated bringing the European Monetary System into being. It established the European Currency Unit (Ecu), its value based on a basket of currencies of member states, as a credit reserve and a means of settlement of official debts amongst Community institutions. Increasingly its use has extended to the private sector. It operates an exchange rate mechanism, within which a central rate for the Ecu is fixed for each participating currency. Permitted fluctuations between most currencies are limited, as in the snake, to 2.25 per cent (Italy's permitted fluctuations are within 6 per cent), with a requirement for national central banks to intervene to maintain the levels. Any devaluation or revaluation of individual currencies can only be fixed jointly by all the participating states.

Genscher–Colombo

The next attempt to restart the process of integration was taken on the initiative of the German and Italian Foreign Ministers Genscher and Colombo, in 1981 (EC Commission 1981). Greece had entered the Community at the beginning of the year and negotiations for the admission of Spain and Portugal were proceeding. There was a growing feeling that, unless the Community was to be further diluted through enlargement, the decision-making process needed to be strengthened. With economic divergences between member states widening, there was a shared sense of urgency to re-examine the state of the Community and its development.

The proposals were directed at the strengthening of Community institutions and extending their competence to foreign policy, security, and cultural affairs. After a year or so of negotiations the Genscher–Colombo Plan was watered down to a solemn declaration issued at the Stuttgart Summit meeting of the Heads of Governments in 1983. This 'reaffirmed their will to transform the whole complex of relations between their States into a European Union'. Without going into specifics, they agreed to the development of a European social policy that, as they said, 'implies in particular the transfer of resources to less prosperous regions; to the strengthening of European Political Co-operation aimed at speaking with a single voice on foreign policy, including political aspects of security; and to the promotion of closer co-operation in cultural matters'. Progress towards these objectives was to be reviewed within five years. Like so many previous declarations, it did not, however, advance its objectives, nor did it clarify the concept of European Union.

The Draft Treaty

The latter task was undertaken within the first directly elected Parliament. In July 1980 Altiero Spinelli founded the 'Crocodile Club', named after a Strasbourg restaurant where supporters of Community reform first met. They formulated a resolution calling on the European Parliament to draw up proposals for institutional reform. In July 1981 the Parliament agreed to the setting up of an Institutional Committee which would have the task of producing a comprehensive draft treaty for the establishment of a European Union. Spinelli was made the Committee's co-ordinating rapporteur, with six other rapporteurs undertaking the drafting of separate aspects of the proposals. After nearly three years' work, the draft treaty was adopted on 14 February 1984 by a large majority representing members from all Community countries and from all political party groups. Out of 311 members present, 237 voted in favour, thirty-one against and forty-three abstained.

The Draft Treaty was comprehensive. It placed within the Union all aspects of policy of concern to the existing Community, as well as foreign affairs, defence, education, research, and cultural matters. In the allocation of responsibilities to the European institutions, it adopted the so-called principle of subsidiarity. This means that the union 'shall only act to carry out those tasks which may be undertaken more effectively in common than by the Member States acting separately'. The areas of competence were divided into two parts – common action and co-operation between states. Common action would normally be taken by majority voting, whereas co-operation would require unanimous agreement.

Exclusive competence was allocated to the Union for all matters concerning the free movement of people, goods, services and capital, trade and competition policy and, after a transitional period, development aid policy. There would be shared competences, with majority voting, in the fields of economic and monetary affairs, as well as in all other sectoral spheres such as agriculture, social, regional, industrial, environmental, educational, and cultural policies. Issues reserved to intergovernmental co-operation were foreign and defence policies. The institutional arrangements of the Draft Treaty were largely based on the existing Community pattern, but a process of co-decision between the Council of Ministers and Parliament would give equal weight to both. In its provisions the Draft Treaty provided for developments of existing Community responsibilities to achieve an efficient and democratically controlled European Union. It furthermore empowered the European Council, by unanimous agreement, to move further towards a full federation, including the transfer of national armed forces to the Union.

After a wide-ranging public campaign in support of the Draft Treaty, President Mitterrand promised the Parliament, during the French presidency of the Council, to examine and support the draft 'with the basic premise to which we agree'. At the Summit held in Fontainebleau in June 1984, Mitterrand persuaded his fellow Heads of Governments to set up an Ad Hoc Committee of their representatives to examine the Draft Treaty and work out proposals for institutional reform. That committee reported a year later to the Milan Summit, which decided to convene an Intergovernmental Conference to negotiate amendments to the existing treaties as well as a treaty on political co-operation.

The Intergovernmental Conference held at the end of 1985, which led to the adoption of the Single European Act in 1986 was the culmination of the process launched by the Parliament and born out of Altiero Spinelli's initiative. It was the first major reform of the treaty that established the European Community, and a giant stride along Europe's road to full union.

Economic, monetary and political union

The latest commitment to progress towards European Union stems from the Single European Act. This laid down a firm decision to proceed to full Economic and Monetary Union and extended the Community's responsibilities to foreign policy and security. The European Council set up a committee under the chairmanship of Commission President Delors whose recommendations are the subject of the intergovernmental conference on Economic and Monetary Union, which started its work at the end of 1990. A parallel intergovernmental conference to work out progress to Political Union is considering the Community's future role in the field of foreign policy and defence and the institutions necessary to operate the Union. The aim of the two conferences is to negotiate treaty reforms or, if necessary, a new Treaty for European Union which, it is hoped, will be ratified by the Community's national parliaments before the end of 1992. The objective is a full European Union in place before the end of this century.

Chapter three

Managing the market

The economic lesson of this century has been that free trade and open markets are a much better recipe for growth and prosperity than national protection and restrictions. The rapid economic growth of the original six member countries of the Community during its first fifteen years, when customs duties and trading barriers were being removed, was a dramatic demonstration of the liberating and dynamic effects of open markets. One of the main aims of the Single European Act is to repeat this experience.

But there is a danger in the belief that removing all barriers to trade is all that is required. 'The market knows best' is a currently fashionable view in some Community countries. So is the view that the less government the better. It is true that national deregulation is required in implementing the Single European Act wherever this conflicts with the objectives of creating a fully integrated European market. This does not, however, mean that market forces need not be regulated and controlled to ensure free and fair competition. The removal of barriers to trade is necessary but that is not all that is needed to achieve a fully integrated market.

Indeed, collective policies complementing free access to the common market are an essential part of the process of integration. The common market is not an end in itself but, as stated in the Treaty setting up the EEC, a means of promoting a continuous and balanced expansion and rapidly rising living standards. If a dynamic and competitive European economy is to be achieved then the Community needs to go beyond a free trade area. That means a common monetary policy leading to a full monetary union. It involves stable and co-ordinated macro-economic policies, including a growing approximation of taxation. The market needs a vigorous competition and mergers policy that promotes efficiency. Finally the Community's external commercial policy must avoid unjustified protectionism and give a lead to the achievement of freer international trade.

Monetary Union

By far the most important contribution to creating a stable, dynamic, and fully integrated market will be macro-economic convergence and exchange-rate stability. That is why achieving a full economic and monetary union has been on the Community's agenda for some twenty years. A treaty commitment to progress towards it has now been written into the Single European Act.

Economic convergence cannot be achieved with floating exchange rates. Earlier, the floating of currencies was welcomed by some countries as an automatic means of dealing with balance of payments problems. It was furthermore believed that it would allow each country greater autonomy in the conduct of its economic policies. In the event, floating currencies have encouraged much more erratic flows of capital, stimulated inflation and impeded growth.

Following the breakdown in the 1970s of the fixed exchange rate system, established by the 1944 Bretton Woods Agreement, the Community has made two attempts to regulate European currencies. The first attempt in 1972, following up the Werner proposals for monetary union, failed, after the world economic crisis in 1973 generated by the explosion of primary commodity prices.

The European Monetary System, set up in 1979, was a much more ambitious project. It established a common currency unit, the Ecu, to which currencies are linked by a central rate within an exchange rate mechanism. Currencies are allowed to fluctuate within ± 2.25 per cent of their central rate (± 6 per cent in the case of Italian lira). The rates can be 'realigned', if necessary, but this can only be done by mutual agreement between participating countries. To help individual currencies to stay within the band, all the central banks are obliged to intervene in the foreign exchange markets. Short-term credit support is also available for countries in difficulties.

The aim of the system was to establish closer monetary co-operation leading to a zone of monetary stability in the European Community. Although Britain, Greece, Portugal, and Spain do not yet belong to it, the record of the exchange rate mechanism is impressive. During a period of massive exchange rate volatility of other world currencies, there have been few alignments between the EMS currencies, and those by relatively small margins. The US dollar and the pound sterling have fluctuated much more wildly.

The EMS was, however, never intended to be an end in itself. Within two years of its creation it was to move into a second phase, which would achieve further monetary integration, including a European Monetary Fund, composed of pooled proportions of member countries' currency and gold reserves. This has not happened, but the Ecu has developed apace and well beyond original expectations.

The Ecu is used for transactions by all Community institutions including the European Investment Bank. By law the Ecu now has the status of a foreign currency in member countries' markets. The private sector has made increasing use of it because of its greater relative stability compared with the individual currencies which form part of it. It is used for bond issues, bank deposits, credit cards, travellers cheques and, increasingly, as a currency for invoicing and for payments. The substantial increase in Ecu exchange transactions, both spot and forward, has also developed its use in international transactions outside the Community. It is now the third most important currency in the international eurobond markets, behind only the dollar and the deutschmark.

A major benefit of the monetary stability brought about by the EMS has been a reduction of the average level of inflation in Europe and a convergence of the economic policies of member states. These have recognized that there is no permanent gain in depreciating the value of their own currency. The most dramatic example of this was the switch in economic policy of the French socialist government which, between 1981 and 1983, pursued a policy of reflation on its own. This led to several damaging devaluations of the French franc and, as a result, a decision to change course. Since 1983 policies pursued in all member countries of the monetary system have followed closely those of West Germany and, as a result, their inflation rates have since converged round the levels traditionally experienced in the Federal Republic.

Recent research has confirmed, not only that the EMS has succeeded in reducing inflation, but that the fall has proved more sustained in the EMS than in non-member countries. Furthermore, contrary to general expectations, greater exchange rate stability was not achieved at the cost of more volatile interest rates.

The success of the EMS and its exchange rate mechanism is bound soon to lead to more currencies joining it. The failure of sterling to join it has been a costly aberration, leading to unnecessarily large fluctuations and instability of its exchange rate, and the need to maintain high interest rates that has damaged the competitive position of British export industries. Most informed opinion within and outside the government had long pressed for British participation. It is likely that, in spite of Mrs. Thatcher's aversion to European interdependence, the integration of the Community's financial markets will force sterling into the system before the end of 1992. The Swiss franc and Austrian schilling are already closely linked, by being virtually pegged to the deutschmark, and when sterling finally joins the exchange rate mechanism Scandinavian currencies are likely to follow suit.

In spite of the greater stability in exchange rates achieved by the monetary system, there are many remaining disadvantages in keeping twelve separate currencies in a market that will soon lose its internal frontiers. A telling example of the cost to individuals of the existence of separate currencies when travelling around the Community was provided in 1987 by Mr. Ben Patterson, a member of the European Parliament. Starting with £100, he 'changed' his money in telephone transactions with each of eleven Community countries successively, ending up with only £55.50, or just over half of the original sum. The exercise done by Mr. Patterson is set out in table 1.

Table 1

Country	Exchanged	Received	£ equivalent
Ireland	£100	105 punts	£100
Portugal	105 punts	2800 escudos	£98.32
Spain	2800 escudos	17.700 pesetas	£91.84
France	17.700 pesetas	800 francs	£85.45
Italy	800 francs	166.500 lira	£84.05
Greece	166.500 lira	16.650 drachma	£83.96
Belgium	16.650 drachma	3.950 francs	£66.44
Netherlands	3.950 francs	205 guilders	£63.47
W. Germany	205 guilders	175 deutschmarks	£61.19
Denmark	175 deutschmarks	640 kroner	£59.26
Britain	640 kroner	£55.50	£55.50

Most countries with traditionally weak currencies used to maintain some form of exchange controls. The decision taken in 1988 to remove them will increase the volume of cross-border capital flows, as the relative values of individual currencies become much more sensitive to changes in expectations. The only effective way to prevent such damaging flows, which would need ever greater intervention by central banks and ever more frequent interest rate changes to prevent excessive movements, must be to make all currencies equally attractive to investors. To do so will require even closer harmonization of monetary policy and the convergence of macro-economic performance among the European economies. Such convergence, coupled with an increasingly unified goods and capital market, will make future re-alignments in currencies no longer necessary.

Indeed, the use of twelve different currencies within the present Community is a clear obstacle to a unified market. Investors and traders do not know what one currency will be worth in terms of another. Individual travellers, as illustrated in table 1, have to pay large dealers' margins as they change money. Much paperwork and costs are also involved in commercial transactions.

These factors will inevitably increase the attractiveness of the Ecu as a parallel currency, both in the public and private sectors. However, if it is to be widely used, it will be ncessary to merge the official and private Ecu and develop it into an actual currency, with notes and coins issued for everyday use. Its basis would also have to be changed from its current dependence on the values of individual member currencies and the US dollar and gold reserves which underpin it.

The wider use of the Ecu as a parallel and official reserve currency will require the establishment of a European Federal or Central Bank. Its primary task would be to issue the Ecu and control its supply and, as it ceases to be a composite currency based on a basket definition, to influence the level of its interest rate. There is growing support amongst member states for such a bank as one of the steps needed for progress towards the agreed objective of an Economic and Monetary Union.

One of the questions to be settled will be the independence of such a federal bank from national governments. Opinion appears to be moving towards creating an autonomous institution with its independence constitutionally guaranteed, operating a European reserve system but with functions which would not allow it to finance deficits either of national governments or of the European Community.

As a result of the creation of the single market there will be, not only increased competition between banks and financial institutions, but a process of competition between national currencies. Anybody in Portugal, for instance, will be able to denominate their assets or liabilities in deutschmarks or any other currency they choose. It will be possible for a business in Britain to settle debts in French francs and to acquire assets in guilders. With complete freedom for individuals and businesses to operate in different currencies, the tendency will be to choose those which are most stable and whose purchasing power is best maintained. This process of competition will inevitably create a demand for a single European currency.

Does the creation of a single European currency, replacing existing national currencies, and its management by a European federal reserve bank, mean the end of national governments and parliaments, as suggested by some, including Mrs. Thatcher? Certainly the adoption of a single currency implies a common monetary policy. It does not, however, necessarily require a unified or even a co-ordinated European fiscal policy, a point which was argued recently in an authoritative report by the deputy director-general of the Banca d'Italia, Tomasso Padoa-Schioppia. In a unified capital market, governments would no longer be able to print their own money to finance deficits but would have to rely on other fiscal measures to maintain their creditworthiness.

It is true, as the President of the European Commission, Jacques Delors, recently suggested that monetary union, secured by a single currency managed by a Community federal bank, would mean transferring substantial economic functions from national to Community level. But experience of other federations, such as the USA, the German Federal Republic, Australia, India, and Switzerland, shows that the individual states within the federations retain considerable powers, which include the right to level their own taxes. Such powers continue to be exercised by state governments, answerable to their own elected parliaments.

Detailed consideration is given in chapter 7 to the way in which powers are distributed between the institutions of the Community and those of its member states, and the nature of the institutions required to exercise any new powers transferred to the Community.

What is surely indisputable, however, is that you can no more have a genuinely unified European market with several currencies operating independently than you could have the states of the USA issuing and managing their own separate currencies. Indeed, a unified market without a European currency would be like a building without foundations.

Taxation

Other barriers to creating a free and competitive internal market need to be removed or reduced. First there is taxation. Whilst customs duties have long been abolished, fiscal barriers continue to hamper free trade. There are divergent national VAT and excise duties. The differing levels of taxation cause divergences in production costs and selling prices. To correct these, member states have to maintain frontier formalities and controls, at which taxes are remitted on exports and imposed on imports. Apart from heavy costs caused by delays and formalities, these differences invite tax evasion and fraud, which are difficult and costly to police.

A uniform level of taxation throughout the Community might seem desirable, but American experience, for instance, shows that this is not necessary. Sales taxes vary between different states within the USA, but in practice they do not diverge by more than 5 per cent, a margin that does not appear to distort trade or prevent its free flow across state boundaries. A similar margin is suggested by the European Commission, which wants VAT and excise duties between member states to be brought to within 6 per cent of each other. The Commission has in mind two rate bands for VAT. The standard rate of between 14 per cent and 20 per cent and a reduced one for basic necessities of between 4 per cent and 9 per cent. Member states would be free to fix the actual levels within these bands. The current standard rate of 15 per cent, applied in Britain, would pose no problems. Similarly the Commission wants rates of excise duties to be approximated.

There has, however, been a lot of resistance from member states to these proposals. The objections stem from both political and revenue considerations. Britain and Ireland operate a zero rate on some items including food, children's clothing, and books. Mrs. Thatcher has threatened a veto on any attempt to prevent zero rating being applied in Britain in the future. For Denmark, reductions in VAT from its present uniform level of 22 per cent to the proposed maximum of 20 per cent and 9 per cent, would reduce overall Danish tax revenue by as much as 7 per cent. Even more drastic reductions would be required to lower the 200 per cent Danish purchase tax levied on cars.

It has been suggested that approximation of taxes will be forced on member countries by the market itself. Leaving it to market forces, however, would invite fiscal competition between states and this – unless frontier barriers were retained – would harm both trade and public revenue. Progressive approximation might be the transitional answer. Temporary exemptions might be permitted for products less sensitive to transnational competition so long as they do not involve continuing frontier controls.

The approximation of excise duties is particularly important in the case of transport. At present much distortion of competition is caused by widely differing diesel, road and vehicle taxes, though here political objections to their harmonization are less likely. In the case of tobacco and alcohol, objections to harmonizing levels are usually based on grounds of health, where they have to be lowered, and on social habits, where they would have to be raised. Progressive approximation within agreed limits over a number of years might be the solution.

Competition policy

The reason for a vigorous competition policy is that it stimulates economic activity, forcing enterprises continuously to improve their efficiency. Furthermore it guarantees free competition by preventing cartels and restrictive agreements. The Treaty of Rome outlaws deals between companies to fix prices, share out markets, place limits on investment, development, and production, or adopt other restrictive practices. It bans abuses of dominant position by firms or groups of enterprises and forbids government subsidies that distort or threaten to distort competition. The policy is administered by the European Commission which has full powers to make sure it is observed.

A few examples will illustrate the way the Commission enforces its competition policy. Market sharing agreements have generally been banned. The first fines imposed by the Commission were in 1969 on companies operating a cartel in quinine. Sugar producers operating a cartel were fined in 1973; and more recently, in 1984, cartels of zinc and flat glass manufacturers were fined a total of Ecu 4 million (£2.7 million).

Price-fixing agreements, such as the dye-stuffs cartel which in 1969 controlled 80 per cent of the European market, were outlawed. Firms with head offices outside the Community were fined because they were operating within the Community in a way damaging to its interests.

There is a ban on agreements to buy only from specified manufacturers or importers, and to sell only to certain buyers, because they carve up the market and give unfair advantages which distort free trade. The products involved range from gramophone records to heating equipment.

Agreements, including those operated in the motor trade which seek to restrict parallel imports, are also outlawed. The Ford motor company was heavily fined for applying such agreements, as was the Moet-Hennessy champagne group, whose British subsidiary banned UK traders from re-exporting its products. Discrimination against retailers, especially for their pricing policies, has also been severely punished.

Even in cases of agreements on industrial and commercial property rights, the exclusive use of patents, trade marks or works of art is not always exempted from competition rules. In 1982, for instance, the Court of Justice ruled against the total territorial protection granted by a patent licensing contract covering maize seed.

The policy is not, however, purely negative, but also encourages positive developments. The Commission has authorized agreements which help to improve the production and distribution of goods, or promote technical or economic progress. Being interested in co-operation between small- and medium-sized enterprises, the Commission allows some types of agreements which escape the general ban. These include: exclusive representation contracts given to trade representatives, small-scale agreements involving a turnover of less than Ecu 50 million (£33 million) with a market share of not more than 5 per cent, sub-contracting agreements, and exchanges of information, joint studies, and joint use of plants between companies.

A major problem of competition policy is that national governments tend to shield national or local firms from competition through state aid, public ownership, preferential public procurement, special loans, export subsidies and loss write-offs. A recent example of the latter was the British Government's attempt to write-off all the accumulated losses of the Rover car company before selling it to the private sector. Many of these practices are being outlawed, but continuous policing by a vigilant Commission is necessary to prevent them happening in spite of their illegality. Disputes can be resolved by the European Court of Justice.

As we move towards a fully integrated market, all mergers between companies which could damage competition and consumer interests in the Community as a whole will have to be policed by the Commission, instead of being left to national governments. In the past the Commission has occasionally intervened, as it did in the take-over of British Caledonian by British Airways. Once the market is integrated there is, however, no further case for national governments to operate their own rules and all mergers that have a European dimension should become a Community responsibility. This should cover mergers above a certain level of turnover which would have to be automatically referred for adjudication by the Commission.

European laws dealing with public companies have been enacted over many years, although proposals for a European Company Statute had, up to 1988, failed to gain approval of member states. Yet, with the full integration of the market, different national legal systems need to be reconciled to allow the formation of genuinely European companies that can operate without hindrance throughout the Community. Many existing directives, laying down common practices, deal with disclosure, capital formation, how assets and liabilities are handled in mergers, take-overs and company closures, and company accounts and their auditing.

The inclusion of workers' rights in the proposed European Company Statute is also unresolved. The reasons for including provisions for workers' rights are twofold. First, working conditions differing substantially from country to country can distort trade and investment. The other is to promote good industrial relations. These should include the right to be informed and consulted over proposed closures, moves, changes in organization and working methods, and the introduction of new technologies. Statutory participation of workers in supervising management in both Germany and The Netherlands has created excellent industrial relations that are the envy of the rest of Europe and ought to provide an example to be followed. In any case, for companies increasingly operating in several member states, the currently divergent rules for worker participation should be harmonized.

External relations

Completing the internal market will require the further development of a common external policy. Separate national policies for dealing with imports from outside the Community could only operate by keeping controls at frontiers to prevent trade distortions and deflections, something which is, of course, incompatible with an internal market in which frontiers have been abolished. Differing quotas, like those applied to Japanese cars, for instance, could no longer be permitted.

There is, however, an even more important case for a common external policy that is open to the rest of the world. If the Community's aim is to promote competitiveness, response to demand, and innovation, then a 'Fortress Europe' approach to trade with the rest of the world would be not only illogical but liable to weaken European economic performance in comparison with its principal world competitors.

Voluntary export restraints negotiated with foreign suppliers by individual member states in the 1970s, have fostered inefficiency, without really being effective, and have been very costly for consumers. Greater competitiveness in the Community's home market is the best way of responding to competitive pressures from the rest of the world. Being the world's largest trader, the Community's overriding interest is to fight protectionism throughout the world. By using its economic weight the Community can enforce reciprocal access and thus stimulate international trade so that everyone benefits.

Chapter four

Technology without frontiers

Advances in technology since the Second World War have made national frontiers increasingly irrelevant. One can no longer effectively separate, isolate or protect nations from each other. Travelling by air one crosses frontiers without being aware of them. With the help of satellites, radio and television can be beamed to all parts of the world. Direct telephone dialling links individuals across whole continents and can be used to send facsimiles of documents instantaneously. Electricity grids, and oil and gas pipelines share out energy across sea and land frontiers. Pollution knows no barriers either. Sea and river pollution by oil or toxic chemicals, acid rain from smoke and radiation from nuclear accidents, like Chernobyl, take no notice of national borders.

The European Community's contribution to technological developments and their commercial exploitation has, however, been patchy and, in many areas, beaten by American, Japanese, Korean, and south-east Asian competition. This has not been due to a lack of scientists of suitable calibre or shortage of resources available for research and development. Indeed, as the Albert–Ball Report, referred to in chapter 1, pointed out, Europe's expenditure on research and development matched that of the USA and was double the Japanese expenditure. The problem has for long been a lack of co-operation between Community members, with each country tending to pursue independent policies that frequently duplicate research and make products that are incompatible with those of their neighbours. As a result, many European products have failed to gain effective entry into international markets that have been dominated by the Americans and Japanese and, increasingly, by South-East Asian producers.

There are, of course, exceptions where European technology has got its act together, as in space and aviation and, due to Jean Monnet's original initiative, in the control of the peaceful use of nuclear power. It has only been since the 1980s that the dangers of European technology being outstripped by its competitors started to alarm industry and

51

governments. Measures since then, described below, have been taken in many fields and there is hope that the Europeans will catch up in due course. Wisely, Community policies have concentrated on enabling and assisting research establishments and industries in both public and private sectors to collaborate across frontiers, and they have not limited such co-operation to Community countries alone.

It is the removal of protectionism in public procurement and the adoption of common standards, envisaged by the Single European Act, that will, however, be the key to the creation of a unified market for technology in Europe. Only then will it match the advantages of large home markets that both America and Japan have for so long enjoyed. A further major stimulus to technological research and development in Europe could also come from the development of a European Security Policy based on common arms procurement; so would learning from the Japanese example of direct government involvement in encouraging research and development co-operation between private firms in civilian markets.

Nuclear power, space, and aviation

The first European attempt to recognize the international dimension of modern technology was the European Atomic Energy Community (EURATOM) set up in 1957 alongside the European Economic Community. It was fathered by Jean Monnet's Action Committee for the United States of Europe. Its proposals were contained in a Memorandum submitted to the Six member governments of the European Coal and Steel Community. The reasons advanced for their proposals were:

An atomic industry producing atomic energy will inevitably be able to produce bombs. For that reason the political aspects and the economic aspects of atomic energy are inseparable. The European Community must develop atomic energy exclusively for peaceful purposes. This choice requires a watertight system of control. It opens the way to general control on a world-wide scale ... The development of atomic energy for peaceful uses opens the prospect of a new industrial revolution and the possibility of a profound change in living and working conditions. Together our countries are capable of themselves developing a nuclear industry. They form the only region in the world that can attain the same level as the great world Powers. Yet separately they will not be able to overcome their time-lag which is a consequence of European disunity.

In short: advanced technology required resources which were beyond the capacity of individual European countries; international control was an important safeguard against the misuse of nuclear energy; and only by acting together could Europe be capable of matching the other world industrial giants.

The most important objectives of the EURATOM Treaty were a nuclear common market, a common programme for research and development, and control over the supply of nuclear fuel. In the event, Euratom's most significant achievement has been the establishment of a Joint Research Centre with sites in several Community countries even though this has been bedevilled by arguments between member states over its funding. Its work is largely concentrated on nuclear safety and environmental protection. The more recent Joint European Torus (JET), set up at Culham in Oxfordshire, undertakes all European research into nuclear fusion. With plentiful supplies of uranium ore, Euratom's role of procuring fuel has, however, become redundant. Furthermore national programmes for both military and civil uses of nuclear energy have been developed independently of EURATOM by several member states.

The second area of European collaboration has been in the field of a space research programme. In 1964 two organizations were set up. One was the European Space Vehicle Launcher Development Organization (ELDO) and the other the European Space Research Organization (ESRO) whose membership included a number of countries belonging to both the European Community and its associated European Free Trade grouping, EFTA. ELDO began the design, development and construction of a launcher using a British rocket as a first stage, a French one for the second, and a German for the third. But the programme was plagued by so many problems that, initially, European satellites, developed by ESRO, had to use American rockets. Ultimately it was agreed to rely on a French design to build the Ariane launcher. Finally in 1975 eleven countries, including Belgium, Denmark, France, Germany, Ireland, Italy, The Netherlands, Spain, Sweden, Switzerland, and the UK set up the European Space Agency (ESA). In 1987 they were joined by Austria and Norway with Finland becoming an associate member.

The European Space Agency's objective is 'to provide and to promote, for exclusively peaceful purposes, cooperation among European states in space research and technology and their space applications, with a view to their being used for scientific purposes and for operational space application systems'. ESA has taken over the role of ELDO and ESRO but its work extends to other areas. Its task is to elaborate a long-term European space policy and to recommend space objectives to member states. It co-ordinates national space programmes with the aim of integrating them ultimately in a common European space programme.

Since its inception the ESA has launched over twenty satellites for scientific purposes, for weather, communications, and television. In 1979 the Ariane rocket successfully completed its first test flight and has since then been launched several times. The launch services of Ariane are now offered world-wide as a reliable and successful space vehicle. Future plans of the ESA include the development of a new generation of powerful launchers, the development of a manned spaceplane Hermes, and ultimately of a space station. Plans include the launching of new satellites for earth observation, science, and telecommunications. Once in orbit, the satellites are leased to the European Telecommunications Satellite Organization (EUTELSAT) operating for twenty-six national PTTs (Posts, Telegraph, and Telephone organizations) and for the European Organization for the Exploitation of Meteorological Satellites (EUMETSAT) representing meteorological agencies of most west European countries.

Although Europe's efforts in space are not inconsiderable, combined national and European expenditure represents less than one-tenth of US and one-fifteenth of Soviet expenditure on space. Indeed European space efforts fall considerably short of a truly effective joint policy that could make Europe an autonomous space power. Europe is not backward scientifically and its financial, technological, industrial, and human potential matches that of the USA or the Soviet Union. There is, however, a continuing fragmentation of effort between national programmes and inadequate financial resources devoted to space activities. As Europe unites it should develop and operate a joint reconnaissance satellite system for safeguarding its political and diplomatic interests and, in self defence, for monitoring arms control verification, military movements, and for crisis control. More of this in chapter 8.

The aviation sector has been another area in which collaboration between European countries has developed satisfactorily. The impact of large-scale US civil and defence aerospace programmes forced European governments to seek collaboration with each other on major aerospace projects. The Anglo-French Concorde was the first major collaborative venture. This co-operation was consolidated by the Anglo-French helicopter and Jaguar projects. By the end of the 1960s European collaboration was extended to the development of the Tornado aircraft by Britain, Germany, and Italy.

At the same time negotiations led to the setting up of Airbus Industrie to produce the European Airbus. The original agreement was signed by France, Germany and Britain, but the British government withdrew, though British industrial participation was assured by private agreement with Airbus Industrie. Dutch and Spanish companies joined the venture later and British Aerospace (BAe) became a full partner in 1979. After initial difficulties the first Airbus, the A300B, turned into a successful venture with sales by 1975 achieving a substantial lead over American competitors in its class. Apart from European sales, non-European orders came from Air India and South African Airways. The next versions, the A310, followed by the A320, were even more successful, being purchased by some forty airlines. By 1986 sales and orders for the different versions totalled some 650 aircraft. Development of the A330/ A340 is going ahead with national public funds backing all the participating industries, including the British.

High technology

Although European countries have been reasonably successful in developing collaborative ventures in the space and aviation sectors, this has not been true of electronics and telecommunications. Europe still suffers from being a diverse collection of nation states, whereas its principal competitors in high technology, the USA and Japan, are single nations with fairly coherent industrial policies. The divisions are compounded by national protection from international competition. In telecommunications, for instance, most European countries maintain national monopolies in public PTTs which normally buy their equipment exclusively from domestic electronics firms. The same applies to the public sector in data processing equipment and above all in defence procurement.

The existence of protected national public sector markets in electronics is the main reason for Europe's relative weakness *vis-à-vis* its main competitors in information technology (IT). Partly this is due to the high cost of research and development for some products. The 1980 generation of digital switching systems required a minimum investment of Ecu 500 million (£333 million) and the next generation to be produced in the 1990s will cost double. With the expected life of switching equipment down from thirty to ten years a supplier must secure at least 8 per cent of the world market to justify the necessary investment in research and development. Only two American firms, AT&T and ITT, have larger shares of the world market. In Europe none reach the minimum figure. The same applies to the production of memory chips, which require massive investment in research and development, though here a number of European firms have the financial capacity to make them.

The above handicaps do not, however, apply to the same extent in other areas of IT. Smaller firms producing computers, software, copiers, etc. are able to sell world-wide but have for a long time been inhibited by the easier options offered in their protected domestic markets. Indeed in the 1960s and 1970s governments deliberately encouraged the creation of so called 'flag-carrying' firms in computers, telecommunications, aerospace, and nuclear energy generation. To move towards national concentration governments intervened to rationalize the domestic industries on the grounds that economies of scale could only support one national firm in the principal sectors. To rely on foreign technology and firms was an admission of economic weakness and decline. As subsequent developments showed, that policy was bound to fail.

The speed of change in high technology, the shorter life of each generation of new products, and consequently the ever higher cost in research and development, has forced world-wide collaboration. New generations of micro-computers, for instance, are launched sometimes within six months of their predecessors. A new commercial aircraft takes five years to develop at a cost of nearly Ecu 2 billion (£1.33 billion). Few national companies in Europe have adequate resources on their own and full mergers or take-overs across national boundaries have proved difficult against the diversity of national regulations, standards, public procurement rules, and chauvinistic resistance. As an alternative, collaboration in high technology has developed across the Atlantic and with Japan and is now much encouraged across European frontiers by governments and European Community institutions.

The European Community recognized that in the development of new technologies no single European country had a sufficiently large research effort or market to meet the challenge. Already, in 1978, the Community launched a programme in Forecasting and Assessment in Science and Technology (FAST) concerned with information technology, the 'bio-society', and the likely transformation of work and employment. This was followed, in 1983, by a four-year FAST 2 programme which was devoted to relations between technology, work, and employment, the development of integrated systems for renewable natural resources, the emergence of new industrial systems in the audio-visual, cable networks, telecommunications, and food processing sectors, and the transformation of service activities and technological change.

In parallel with the FAST 2 programme, the European Community launched a plan for the transnational development of infrastructure to assist innovation and technology transfer. After a first three year phase, this was extended, in 1986, under a new name, SPRINT (Strategic Programme for Innovation and Technology Transfer). The innovation programme was directed particularly to helping small and medium-sized enterprises which, unlike larger companies, need skilled support for research and development of new products, and their marketing, especially on a transnational basis.

As a result of growing concern amongst industrialists about Europe's relative decline in information technology a whole change of direction came in the early 1980s. European firms supplied a mere 40 per cent of the Community's domestic market and about 10 per cent of the world's. In response, European Commissioner Davignon organized a series of Round Table discussions with leading electronics and IT companies. A steering committee was established which, in 1982, resulted in a Commission proposal to the Council of Ministers to set up a European Strategic Programme for Research and Development in Information Technology (ESPRIT). A pilot scheme was agreed which led to some thirty-eight collaborative contracts with participants in at least two or three members states. Firms in the pilot scheme included twenty-seven British, twenty-one German, ten Dutch, eight Belgian, four French, and two Italian. Costs were shared equally between the European Community and industry.

Once the pilot scheme was under way the Commission submitted a full ten-year ESPRIT programme (1984–93). In the first five years this was to concentrate research on micro-electronics, advanced information processing, and software technology, and their application to office systems and computer integrated manufacturing. The proposals were approved and, after evaluation, 201 projects were selected involving 240 firms and 210 research institutions. The programme was defined by a specially created Task Force for Information Technology and Telecommunications and is now managed by the European Commission under the guidance of an ESPRIT Advisory Board and Management Committee. The cost of the first five-year phase approached Ecu 1.5 billion (£1 billion). The second five-year programme, with a budget of Ecu 2 billion, is going to be three times as extensive as ESPRIT 1 and its main areas of research will be micro-electronics, IT processing systems and application technologies.

The spin-off from the ESPRIT programme has been pressure for the rationalization of European IT standards for open communication networks. These include message handling, teletext, documents exchange, and the development of common programming languages and technical descriptions. Agreements have been reached on the exchange of information between member countries and on planned draft standards which has led to the mutual recognition of type approvals for telecommunications terminal equipment and to the setting up of European IT and telecommunications conformity testing services.

In the field of telecommunications the Community launched another programme called RACE (Research and Development in Advanced Communications Technologies for Europe). This required the consent of and close collaboration with national PTTs, with the aim of achieving coherence of the different telecommunication systems and services being developed in Europe. Its more specific objective is the gradual establishment of a Community-wide infrastructure and services based on a common IBCN (Integrated Broadband Communications Network).

The ESPRIT and RACE programmes are being supplemented by a series of complementary programmes on the application of information and telecommunications technologies to cover banking and finance services (DIME), the use of informatics in road traffic (DRIVE), medical information (AIM), and teaching through computers (DELTA).

Industrial technologies

The application of the new technologies in industry was entrusted to another programme called BRITE (Basic Research in Industrial Technologies for Europe). This was launched in 1985 with particular reference to such industries as automobiles, aeronautics, textiles, and chemicals. Another vast new development has been that of biotechnology with its application to agriculture, food processing, the chemical and pharmaceutical industries, the production of bio-mass energy, and the recovery of waste. About 40 per cent of manufactured goods are biological in origin and it is estimated that by the year 2000 the world market for biotechnology will exceed Ecu 100 billion (£67 billion). To help the Community to compete with the USA and Japan, where highly ambitious research and development programmes have outstripped European efforts, the combination of efforts by individual Community countries and development on a continental scale is absolutely crucial. Furthermore, an effective Community programme could help the Third World in becoming self-sufficient in food production and assist it in health care.

To meet this challenge the European Community first introduced the Biomolecular Engineering Programme (BEP) which ran from 1982 to 1985. This was succeeded by a more ambitious Biotechnology Action Programme (BAP) which, in addition to its original concentration on enzyme, genetic, and protein engineering, has two main objectives, namely to promote basic research and training and to promote biotics (the building of cell and gene banks) and bio-informatics or data banks.

It was the announcement by President Reagan in 1983 of his intention to create a Strategic Defence Initiative (SDI), commonly referred to as Star Wars, that really caused concern in Europe. Its technological implications, with billions of dollars flowing into high technology research and development sectors, would inevitably lead to the widening of the gap between America and Europe. One response was the launch, at the initiative of the French government, of the European Research Co-ordinating Agency known as EUREKA. Unlike the American initiative devoted to the defence effort, EUREKA is primarily a programme for civil research. Its aims are identifying, supporting, and co-ordinating non-military industrial projects to enhance European competitiveness and prevent the diversion of human and industrial resources which SDI would otherwise tend to attract from Europe.

EUREKA is backed by all the Community countries as well as by Austria, Finland, Norway. Sweden, Switzerland, and Turkey. It covers several programmes dealing with large computers, third generation robots, automated factories and lasers, research networks and equipment, ceramic turbines and high speed trains, and the integration of high technologies in factories and their adaptation in the home. Other EUREKA programmes are aimed at accelerating the process of formulating European standards, establishing tax incentives for the creation of 'European' firms, and developing a common policy in relation to public procurement markets.

Indeed EUREKA appears to cover practically all the new technologies, many of which seem to overlap existing Community research and development programmes such as ESPRIT, BRITE, BAP, and others. Well over 100 individual projects have been agreed. However, only limited public finance has been made available from individual governments and from the European Community, with most of the funding being left to private sources, either from the firms' own funds or from the capital markets. There are criticisms that the distribution of projects between member states is uneven and that technology transfer will not follow from participation because normal commercial conditions will apply. Whilst individual projects will no doubt be worthwhile, the total programme does not match the USA's technology push of which SDI forms an important part. American public spending on research and development outstrips those devoted to EUREKA by nearly 100 to 1.

Technological Community

It is clear that on its own EUREKA will not be the complete answer to the technological challenge faced by Europe. The concept of a European Technological Community, on the other hand, centred on the European Community would give a much more coherent framework for various strands of Community activity and also provide an effective bridge between national, Community and extra Community research and development activities. Recognizing this, the Community launched in 1984 its first framework programme for research and technological development. The idea was incorporated in the Single European Act which, in article 130, states that 'The Community's aim shall be to strengthen the scientific base of European industry and to encourage it to become more competitive at international level'. The second framework programme which runs from 1987 to 1991 is already based on the Single European Act.

The framework programme, designed for medium-term planning, sets general objectives and priorities, provides the overall financial allocation, and determines its breakdown between the major areas of activity. It aims to meet the twin challenge of strengthening Europe's competitiveness in high technology as against the USA and Japan and of improving the cohesion of European economic development. The purpose of cohesion is to reduce existing disparities between member states in the scientific field by ensuring that all countries participate in high-level research.

The underlying philosophy is not the transfer to the Community of most of the research carried out but to ensure that research, which, for one reason or another, can be more economically, more efficiently, or more appropriately conducted at Community level, is so undertaken. This is particularly relevant in areas such as environmental protection and health, and research which exceeds the financial or manpower resources of individual member states, as for instance in the case of thermonuclear fusion. The framework programme singles out eight major lines of activity in the research and technology field.

The first is concerned with the quality of life affected by health and the environment. In the field of health the main thrust is to co-ordinate medical research dealing with cancer and AIDS. Another programme is concerned with protection against radiation and with occupational medicine in the coal and steel industries. In the environmental field the Community is concerned with protection against the build-up of pollutants and acid rain, and the conservation of historic buildings. It also backs research into the so-called greenhouse effect on the climate, caused by the accumulation of carbon dioxide in the atmosphere and the deterioration of the ozone layer.

The second covers information technologies and incorporates several Community programmes such as ESPRIT and RACE. The third area is concerned with new technologies in industry, including the development and production of new materials, research into raw materials and their exploration, mining technology, recycling of waste, the use of wood, etc.

The fourth covers the three principal forms of energy: first, nuclear fission including the safety of reactors, the management and disposal of radioactive waste, and the decommissioning of nuclear power plants at the end of their useful lives; the second one deals with controlled thermonuclear fusion energy in which Europe is a world leader in its JET programme and which promises to become the principal form of energy in the next century; the third deals with non-nuclear energy. This covers technologies for the production, transport, and exploitation of energies such as solar, wind, biomass, geothermal, and of fossil fuels, including the liquefaction and gasification of coal.

The fifth area covers the use of biological resources. The sixth deals with research into the application of science and technology to the problems of the Third World, including agriculture and tropical medicine. The seventh covers marine resources. It is aimed at increasing knowledge of the oceanic environment and at work concerned with the exploration of the sea bottom and its mineral resources, fishing, and aquaculture.

The eighth and last heading within the framework programme covers several activities which contribute to the more speedy establishment of the 'Europe of science and technology'. It embraces advanced research projects in the fertile areas which occur at the meeting point of different disciplines, e.g. the so-called BRAIN project in the area of neuro-informatics, the optimal exploitation of the major European scientific installations, a research programme in the field of automatic translation, and the effective dissemination of the results of all Community research, including publications, data banks, etc.

Supplementing the framework programme is the effective training of people for the new technological age. To do this a programme of the Community in education and training for technology called COMETT was launched in 1987. There is a massive shortage of high level engineers and skilled technicians demanded by the new technologies. The shortage is particularly striking compared to the numbers available in the USA and Japan. Indeed in a number of areas the shortage of highly qualified personnel is an even more serious problem than the lack of finance for development or production costs.

The COMETT programme has several objectives. It encourages synergy between industry and academia. It promotes a European identity by placing students in firms located in other member states. It encourages economies by the joint organization of new training programmes. It improves the initial training of students and develops the levels of training of skilled personnel and executive staffs in response to technological and social changes. It strengthens and diversifies possibilities for training at local, regional, and national levels and exploits opportunities offered by the new information and communication technologies.

Future developments and challenges

What of the future? Within twenty years technology will eliminate geography as a significant factor in our lives. The linking of computers and telecommunications will bring about audio-visual instant communication across the world into practically every home. Electronic mail and messages will largely replace traditional posts. Machine translation and simultaneous interpretation at the receiving end will make world-wide television accessible in all countries in their own languages. Travel will be faster, with space as an added dimension to intercontinental travel. The work-place will normally be at home with the majority engaged in service industries while robotics will largely control production. Most markets will no longer have locations but be based on network communications. Finally information on practically every topic will be instantly accessible in the home through teletext links with databanks.

These and other developments, thanks to advanced technology, will tend, during the twenty-first century, to turn our planet into a global village, but the road to that goal may well be bumpy. Ideally we would need unrestricted transfer of technology and a world market where protection has all but disappeared. Whilst, laudably, we are going in this direction within Europe by removing national barriers and protectionism within the Community, the same is not as true of Europe's principal competitors the USA and Japan.

The Americans jealously guard their technology as the repeated extraterritoriality issues over COCOM (Co-ordinating Committee for East–West Trade Policy) controls frequently illustrate. The Siberian gas pipeline project linking the source to customers in western Europe, which the US tried to stop, was only one of many such attempts to interfere with free trade in technologically advanced products. The buy American policy discriminates against exporters to the USA. Finally the massive procurement programmes confined almost exclusively to American industry by the US defence department and space programmes, have been a major source of American technological superiority, not just in defence or space related equipment but, as a spin off, in most industries using technologies first developed as a result of defence and space contracts. The American home market of 234 million provides a massive base for the growth of large companies that, through takeovers and mergers, have become multinational giants operating on a world-wide scale, not least in Europe itself.

The Japanese technological success does not stem from military research and development. Much of their success came from the encouragement given to private industry by the Japanese Ministry of International Trade and Industry (MITI) to exploit civilian markets. By co-ordinating their activities, with relatively limited financial aid, MITI persuaded Japanese companies to make a large commitment to new product development and to the capture of markets overseas. With a much larger proportion of GNP devoted to research and development than in the western economies, the resulting technological achievements have been most impressive. Operating from a large domestic base of some 119 million consumers, Japanese industry has been highly successful in penetrating markets throughout the world and particularly those of its principal competitors. At the same time, the Japanese have not been averse to protecting their domestic market from foreign incursions by various administrative measures as well as by fostering chauvinist attitudes to imports that are in direct competition with home produced goods.

Europe's interests are not to cut itself off from the rest of the world but, equally, the Community should be just as ready as the USA or Japan to act on occasion in self-interest. Whilst technological collaboration with American, Japanese, and other foreign or multinational firms should not be excluded, the Community should be ready to discriminate against non-European multinationals within its collaborative programmes, just as the Americans and Japanese discriminate against foreign firms. Ultimately all such discrimination ought to disappear, but that will only be achieved on a basis of reciprocity.

Europe's capacity to match the competition will, however, depend on the successful unification of the internal market including public procurement and the achievement of unified regulations and standards in the high-technology fields. As in the USA, these measures must, however, be combined with vigilant and tough anti-trust action. The Community must act forcefully to prevent cartels and the exploitation of dominant market positions which cushion firms from effective competition, weaken their will to innovate, and stifle the more dynamic smaller firms with new ideas. Indeed Europe should encourage new entrants by positive discrimination in awarding public contracts to the smaller firms and ensuring that adequate new venture capital is available to them.

Finally, more public financial resources ought to be made available. A major fillip to Europe's technological effort could come from common arms procurement and a Community defence budget, recommended in chapter 8. The American experience of technological innovation, spearheaded and stimulated by space and defence procurement, provides a telling example of how to keep up the momentum. Once Europe catches up with her main technological rivals, it will be easier to lower barriers between them and, together, spread the benefits of the new technological revolution throughout the world.

Chapter five

Policies for cohesion

Removing national frontiers and creating a single barrier-free market could have damaging economic and social consequences for the weaker regions and sectors of society. This has been explicitly recognized in the Single European Act. In it a whole section is devoted to promoting and strengthening economic and social cohesion so as to ensure the Community's overall harmonious development. In particular it aims to reduce disparities between the various regions of the Community and the backwardness of the least-favoured ones. Another section, devoted to social policy, requires member states to pay particular attention to encouraging improvements, especially in the working environment. The same commitment is made to improving health and the physical environment.

The importance of the social and regional aspects of European integration was recognized from the very beginning. The Treaty of Rome, setting up the European Economic Community in 1957, committed the signatories to the improvement of the living and working conditions of their peoples and to reducing differences between the regions of the Community. Indeed, the concept of economic and social cohesion is accepted as fundamental to all progress towards European unity. To ensure that cohesion within European society is never lost sight of, one of the Community's statutory institutions to be set up has been the Economic and Social Committee, which must be consulted by the Commission and Council on most matters. Its composition is based on three groups: the first covers employers, the second workers and trade unions, the third includes other interest groups such as consumers, farmers, the self-employed, academics, etc. The Committee's work is undertaken by its specialist sections whose recommendations are submitted for approval by the whole Committee in plenary session. The opinions arrived at must be taken into account by the Commission and Council before Community legislation is enacted. The specialist sections cover such diverse subjects as agriculture, transport, energy, economic and financial questions, industry, commerce, the crafts and services, social questions, regional development, protection of the environment, public health, consumer affairs, and external relations.

In all progress towards European unity there has to be a trade-off between the benefits to industry and commerce of a common market and the likely disadvantages to the weaker regions or sectors of society in a free-for-all environment if integration is to be acceptable to the poorer countries and to the public generally. The maintenance of a balance of advantage has thus been an essential condition of all integration.

Criticisms by Mrs. Thatcher, in 1988, of the Community's involvement in legislating for workers' rights, for example, had failed to recognize that these are as much part of the process of integration as the removal of barriers to trade within the Community. Similarly no other member government shares Mrs. Thatcher's objections to the full involvement of trade unions in the consultative process, or her reservations about the social dimension of integration.

Agriculture

The first example of a trade-off in benefits was implicit in the agreement to develop a common agricultural policy. The French, fearing the more powerful and efficient German industry, insisted on a balancing benefit to the agricultural sector, so important to the French economy. But there was a wider consideration which persuaded the EEC's six member states to give priority to agriculture. In the 1950s nearly one third of the Community's population was working and dependent on the land. Their living standards were no more than two thirds of average incomes. Yet farm production was far from satisfying the full demand for foodstuffs, which had to be supplemented by substantial imports from abroad.

To deal with these problems the common agricultural policy was devised to increase agricultural productivity, ensure a fair standard of living for those working on the land, stabilize markets and guarantee regular supplies, and ensure reasonable and stable prices to consumers. The CAP has been largely successful in achieving its objectives, though with some adverse consequences not originally foreseen.

Generous price support to farmers and technical innovation have resulted in massive increases in productivity and supplies. Attracted by higher earnings in industry and with financial help from the Community, more than two thirds of the farming population has abandoned agriculture, whilst the average living standards of those remaining has risen sharply. The Community has become virtually self-sufficient in all but tropical foodstuffs and some animal feeds. The policy has assured price stability, though at a level generally higher than on the world market. From the consumers' point of view supplies have been secure and prices stable, untouched by periodic surges in the world

65

price for sugar and cereals. Indeed, food prices in the Community have risen more slowly than the general price index and, with higher living standards generally, food now accounts for a much smaller proportion of people's domestic budgets than it did when the CAP was started. Food then took about 30 per cent of average budgets, whereas now the figure is less than 20 per cent.

The success of the CAP has, however, had its own costs. The system depends on guaranteed prices for most products, set each year by farm ministers. They are under continuous pressure from their own farmers to set prices at the highest possible level, which in turn stimulates production in excess of current demand. Under the CAP's guarantee system the surpluses have to be taken into stock and from time to time massive so-called 'butter mountains' and 'wine lakes' have been built up. Storage and disposal of the excesses has added to the budget substantially. So have the payments of export subsidies to enable European produce to be sold outside the Community at ruling world prices.

There have been justified protests from competing exporters from the USA, Argentina, Australia, New Zealand, and others about the Community dumping agricultural produce on world markets. Furthermore subsidized sales and food gifts have tended to inhibit Third World countries from developing their own agriculture.

The cost of export subsidies has at times taken up to 40 per cent of the Community's guarantee fund, whereas the total CAP budget has on average absorbed about two-thirds of the whole Community budget. Pressure to reform the CAP has consequently been growing strongly ever since 1969; and there has been some progress, although radical change has been held up by very effective national farming lobbies and the past practice of seeking unanimous agreement amongst ministers.

The difficulties over reforming the CAP have, incidentally, thrown into sharp relief the weaknesses of the Community's decision making. Ministers of agriculture have defended national interests at the Community's expense, as they were not responsible for the budgetary costs. Insistence on unanimity over decisions usually resulted in compromises with little regard to cost. Proposals for reforms, regularly submitted by the Commission, have been either ignored or heavily watered down. Agriculture, the first major common policy, highlighted the fact that you cannot effectively operate policies at European level if narrower national interests take precedence over the common good.

Facing an overall budget crisis, the February 1988 European Council was finally forced to take the problem in hand. Ceilings were imposed on practically all farm products and, as soon as farmers exceed them, automatic price cuts come into force. Total spending on the CAP was frozen and, if the budget is insufficient to make ends meet, the

Commission is empowered to impose even more drastic price cuts.

In the light of these decisions it now looks much more likely that, over a period, agricultural supply will be more closely matched with actual demand, not just within the Community but in world markets too. At the same time there are bound to be losers amongst the farming community and it is here that the CAP budget's guidance section can be of major help. This, amongst other aids, finances programmes to help less favoured regions and mountainous and hilly areas, where it is desirable to keep farmers on the land and avoid depopulation. Other help is also made available from the European Regional Development Fund and the European Investment bank, referred to below.

Regional policy

The development of a regional policy followed the first enlargement of the Community from six to nine members, when Britain, Ireland, and Denmark joined. The Commission found that there was considerable disparity between the poorest and most prosperous regions in each member country and within the Community as a whole. The disparity between the most prosperous and the least developed regions in the present Community of twelve, measured in terms of employment and production, is about five to one. The less privileged regions in the Community now account for more than a quarter of its population and fall into two main groups.

First there are the underdeveloped rural areas, largely dependent on agriculture. Incomes are low, unemployment high, and most suffer from poorly developed infrastructures. They include most of Greece, Ireland, and Portugal, southern Italy and Spain, Corsica and the French overseas departments. The second group covers areas where former prosperity was founded on industries which are now in decline. These are characterized by high unemployment, decaying housing, and social deprivation. They are concentrated in Belgium, Britain, and France.

The Community's policy has three main objectives. First to co-ordinate the regional policies of the member states. Second to ensure that regional problems are fully taken into account in other Community policies. Third to provide broad financial aid towards the development of the Community's poorer regions.

The co-ordination of national policies involves making certain that member states do not engage in the self-defeating practice of outbidding each other by increasing the level of national aid. Upper limits on state aids are fixed and common rules are laid down for a more coherent pattern of regional development and to avoid the waste of scarce resources.

Regional, economic and social factors are interdependent, and this calls for constant examination of the regional consequences of all Community policies. This applies in particular to the CAP, which was found to favour the more prosperous agricultural areas, and to other sector policies dealing with fisheries, ship-building, steel and textiles. The Social Policy and Fund have also been directed towards the needy regions.

The main element of the Community's regional policy is financial support. This comes principally from the European Regional Development Fund and from the European Investment Bank, but also from other structural aid facilities, which direct large sums towards the problems of the poorer and priority regions.

The latter includes help from the Guidance section of the European Agricultural Fund for the modernization of food production and marketing. Since its inception it has given aid in excess of Ecu 10 billion (£6.7 billion). Grants and loans from the European Social Fund and the European Coal and Steel Community, totalling some Ecu 30 billion (£20 billion), have been devoted to the training and retraining of workers for the modernized coal and steel industries, and to attracting new job-creating investments. A New Community Instrument, established in 1979, provides loans for modernizing infrastructure, developing energy resources, and helping small- and medium-sized businesses. The NCI has provided nearly Ecu 6 billion (£4 billion) in loans over and above the help given by the European Investment Bank.

The European Investment Bank was established under the EEC Treaty specifically to finance capital investment aimed at promoting the balanced development of the Community. Up to 1986 it had lent over Ecu 42 billion (£28 billion) of which about two thirds was for developing less prosperous regions.

But the most important redistributive function is exercised through the European Regional Development Fund. Since its creation in 1975 and by 1986 it has distributed nearly Ecu 18 billion (£12 billion) for the promotion of economic activity and improvement of infrastructure in regions qualifying for Community aid. In the first ten years 91 per cent of ERDF spending went to five countries including Britain, France, Greece, Ireland, and Italy. After 1985 rules were changed to allocate the funds between all Community countries on a percentage basis, directed towards the least favoured regions, with the bulk going to the poorest countries – which now include Portugal and Spain. Expenditure from the ERDF accounts for 50 per cent to 55 per cent of total costs, the rest being contributed by member states.

There are two types of programmes aided by the ERDF. There are the Community programmes designed to help solve serious social and economic difficulties in one or more regions. They group projects spread over several years aimed specifically at Community objectives and policies. Many cover help on a cross-border basis affecting several states. The others are for national programmes which fulfil the Community's objectives. The proposals are submitted by the member states, with the bulk of the money being allocated to individual projects put forward on behalf of local authorities, public organizations, or private commercial firms.

Any major changes in policies, size, or structure of the Community have their regional and social implications. In 1986, when Spain and Portugal's entry into the Community became imminent, it was recognized that regions of member states with similar and competing economies might be disadvantaged by the removal of the preferences which, within their own countries, they had previously enjoyed. To deal with the problems the Community introduced Integrated Mediterranean Programmes designed to help regions largely dependent on Mediterranean agricultural produce such as olive oil, wine, fruit, vegetables, etc. The IMPs apply to the whole of Greece and southern parts of France and Italy. The Community is devoting Ecu 6.6 billion (£4.4 billion) over seven years to the IMPs. Together with contributions from national and regional sources IMPs will help them to restructure their farming, diversify their economy, and create new industrial and service jobs, especially for the young.

For the same reason – and to meet the new challenges of the barrier-free internal market and correct the economic imbalances between the richer and poorer countries that may result from the single market – the February 1988 European Council meeting agreed to double, over a five year period, the structural funds aimed at the poorest areas of the Community. This was the trade-off necessary to ensure that the four poorest member states, Greece, Ireland, Portugal, and Spain, joined in constructing the single internal market.

There are two major criticisms of the Community's existing regional policies. The first and most obvious is that the financial and manpower resources which the Community is able to devote to the ERDF and its objectives are hopelessly inadequate to correct in any significant way the enormous disparities which still exist between its regions. Redistribution of wealth between regions requires much more far-reaching measures through the development of a Public Finance Union, of which more below. The other concerns the use and application of the grants received by the member states for projects to assist their regions. They are supposed to be additional to the aid given by national exchequers. Yet all too often they merely replace what governments would have provided out of their own coffers. Indeed the so-called 'additionality' is in reality just a myth.

Social policy

The social policy is designed to facilitate the free movement of labour, a basic principle of the Community, and to promote equal opportunities, to improve working conditions and worker participation, to promote training and education and, above all, to increase employment. Its principal instrument is the European Social Fund whose role during the economic boom period of the 1950s and 1960s was largely limited to the retraining of workers displaced through structural changes.

With the sixfold increase in unemployment between 1970 and 1986, rising to some 16 million or 12 per cent of the working population, the role of the policy and fund became much more significant. Extra resources were devoted to it, so that by 1986 some 7 per cent of the Community budget was allocated to the ESF, equivalent to a five-fold increase over the previous ten years.

The ESF has now two main priorities. First there are the young people under twenty-five for whose training and employment the Fund now spends 75 per cent of its resources. Second there are the most disadvantaged regions. Close to half of the expenditure is concentrated in seven absolute priority areas located in Greece, Ireland, Italy, Portugal, Spain and the French overseas departments.

The fight against unemployment is also directed towards easing economic difficulties resulting from structural changes due to declining industries, technological modernization, or fundamental changes in demand. Help is given for retraining workers, vocational training for the long-term unemployed, and towards job creation initiatives.

Another major concern of the social policy is the assurance of equal opportunities for women. Women are disadvantaged as against men both in employment, where equality of working conditions is still a long way from being achieved, and in female unemployment, which is higher than that of the male population. The Treaty of Rome expressly laid down equal pay for equal work. Since then new legislation has added the right to equal treatment in access to employment, training, promotion, and working conditions. Furthermore, all discrimination in social security legislation is now forbidden. Positive measures are encouraged to change attitudes and attract women to occupations where they are underrepresented and to higher levels of responsibility.

Improving working conditions is another major task of the Community. This involves health, safety and the working environment generally. One aim is to safeguard the rights of workers affected by mass redundancies. This could cover the payment of salaries and such claims as transfer costs to other locations or occupations. Another is the better organization of working time, including such objectives as limiting overtime, encouraging flexible voluntary retirement, and dealing with part-time and temporary work.

The free movement of labour, guaranteed under the Treaty, now applies to all occupations, except for those in the public sector concerned with security, and law and order functions. To improve conditions for migrants, national social security systems have been co-ordinated. Rights of association of migrants have been guaranteed. Teaching the mother tongue, and the culture of young people's country of origin, is now an obligation and Community help is being considered to improve housing conditions for migrants.

The Community also concerns itself with helping the disabled who account for some 10 per cent of the population. It helps to promote the training and employment of disabled people, improve their participation in social life, and aid their mobility by modifying living accommodation and access to buildings.

Despite highly developed social security systems, some 30 million people are estimated to be living in dire poverty in the Community. Amongst them are old people, single-parent families, migrants, long-term unemployed, and other marginal groups. A number of Community programmes have been started to help alleviate their poverty.

The objectives of the social policy can, however, only be achieved through the active involvement of both sides of industry. This involves increased participation by workers in decision-making in their firms, especially in the case of multinational corporations, by obliging them to keep employees and their representatives regularly informed, and to consult them before any decisions are taken that could affect their interests. Apart from the Economic and Social Committee, the dialogue between the so-called social partners is institutionalized within the Commission's Standing Committee on Employment and in various working groups set up to study the effects of Community policies on growth and employment.

The Community Charter of Fundamental Social Rights for Workers (EC Commission 1990), adopted by the European Council in December 1989 by all Community members except the UK, spells out in detail the objectives of the social dimension in the construction of the Single Market. It includes some fifty proposals which will be brought forward by the European Commission before the end of 1992 for their adoption by the member states. These aim at developing the economic and social cohesion of the unified market.

Environment

Alongside concern for better working conditions, the Community is also responsible for protecting and improving the living environment. The

71

legacy of past neglect due to lack of concern over the misuse of natural resources, bad planning, and overdevelopment is still with us. Air, water and soil pollution, noise, and thoughtless destruction of our fauna and flora have finally brought home the recognition that we must preserve the environment.

The Community's concern springs from the obvious fact that the natural environment recognizes no man-made frontiers. Industrial waste and polluted air-streams travel across Europe. Oil slicks can affect any national coastline. Lakes and rivers extending beyond national boundaries can carry poisonous chemicals. Protection of migratory birds in one country is meaningless if they are slaughtered in another.

A common environment policy was first proclaimed at the Community's summit meeting in 1972. This was followed by three consecutive action programmes covering a wide range of measures. These include: the consideration of the impact on the environment of all other Community policies; the prevention and reduction of atmospheric, water or soil pollution; action against noise nuisances; management of waste and dangerous chemical substances and processes; promotion of clean technologies; preservation and, where possible, restoration of the natural environment and habitats needed by both fauna and flora; cross frontier anti-pollution co-operation within Europe and with other parts of the world. Since its start the Community has adopted over 100 legislative acts on the environment.

To prevent water pollution minimum quality standards have been set for sea bathing, for drinking water, and for fresh and sea water suitable for fish and shellfish life. Discharge of toxic substances is strictly controlled. The Community is a signatory and participant of several international conventions aimed at reducing pollution in international waterways such as the Atlantic, the North Sea, the Mediterranean, and international rivers like the Rhine.

Anti-air-pollution measures have covered the discharge of sulphur dioxide, the use of chlorofluorcarbons in aerosol cans which can damage the earth's ozone layer, and the control of pollution from industrial premises. Member states were persuaded to accept the reduction in the lead content of petrol. Agreement has, however, been more difficult to achieve over the control of pollution from large combustion plants, particularly power stations, as well as gases from motor vehicles, which have been the main culprits of the widespread damage to forests through acid rain.

Maximum noise levels have been fixed for all types of motor vehicles, tractors, subsonic aircraft, lawnmowers, and building site machinery. Further proposals are being considered for helicopters and railway vehicles.

Since the disastrous contamination by toxic dioxin in Seveso, northern Italy, stringent measures have been taken to reduce the risks which could stem from the manufacture and disposal of chemical substances. The packaging and labelling of dangerous substances is strictly laid down. Directives control the composition of detergents, pesticides and the use of asbestos.

The collection, disposal, recycling, and processing of waste is similarly subject to Community rules. Special measures apply to the control and disposal of oil and radioactive waste.

Finally several measures have been adopted to conserve wildlife, to ban imports of products made from skins of baby seals, and to control and restrict scientific experiments on animals. Financial support is given to projects to conserve natural habitats and further measures are planned to protect endangered species.

On the increasingly accepted principle that 'the polluter pays', Community money has been concentrated on financing pilot and research projects, conferences, seminars, and technical reports based on studies which would assist the protection of the environment. Community financial resources devoted to these ends have been modest. The current programme of research has some Ecu 50 million (£33 million) at its disposal. Much more substantial funds have, however, been available from the European Investment Bank by way of loans. All public and private projects which help to protect the environment are eligible, regardless of their location. In 1986 for example over Ecu 700 million (£470 million) was lent for environmental projects.

Financing cohesion

Financing all the policies described above, aimed at greater cohesion within the Community, has taken the lion's share of the Community budget. In 1987, for instance, out of a total Community budget of Ecu 38.7 billion (£25.8 billion) agricultural, regional, and social policies absorbed 79 per cent. The European Investment Bank's lending in the same year exceeded Ecu 7 billion (£4.67 billion), with the bulk going to support policies for cohesion. The sums appear large, yet they represent less than 3 per cent of total public expenditure by the twelve member states out of their national budgets, or only about 1 per cent of the Community's gross domestic product.

Until 1988 the budget revenue consisted of four separate elements. These were: customs duties on products imported from outside the Community, agricultural levies charged on imports of foodstuffs to bring their prices up to Community levels, levies on foodstuffs intended to limit overproduction within the Community, and a proportion of value added tax which was raised to 1.4 per cent of VAT in 1986.

The new financial system adopted by the European Council in February 1988 raised the ceiling for Community funding to 1.2 per cent of GDP for payments and 1.3 per cent for commitments undertaken, or a possible budget of Ecu 60 billion (£40 billion). In addition to the VAT element, contributions from member states are adjusted in accordance with their share of total GDP. Expenditure on agriculture has finally been capped and will not be allowed to increase by more than 74 per cent of average GDP growth. Any excess will result in a reduction of prices. At the same time spending on regional and social policies will double by 1993.

The reform of the financial system lies in the adjustments made to VAT contributions to take account of the relative levels of wealth of member states – by linking payments to each country's GNP. This is the first significant tilt away from the Alice-in-Wonderland world in which poorer member countries are net payers while richer are net receivers, in which poorer farmers pay for richer ones and in which highly developed regions are more favoured than the less favoured ones.

The reform may thus be the very first step in the development of a European Public Finance Union, which is an essential accompaniment to the proposed economic and monetary union. When the Community originally decided in 1972 to work towards an economic and monetary union by 1980, the Commission set up a high-level study group, under the chairmanship of Sir Donald MacDougall, to look at the role of public finance in such a union. The MacDougall Report, published in 1977, looked first at existing economic unions including five federations (Australia, Canada, Germany, Switzerland, and the USA) and three unitary states (France, Italy, and the United Kingdom) and compared them with the Community (EC Commission 1977).

These showed that public expenditure by members of the Community averaged about 45 per cent of the GNP, whereas Community expenditure was under 1 per cent. In federal countries public expenditure at federal level, as distinct from lower levels of government, ranged between 20 per cent and 25 per cent. It found that inequality between richer and poorer member states of the Community is at least as great as regional inequalities in income levels within the above eight countries studied, before allowing for the redistributive effects of public finance. Within these countries the redistributive effect of public expenditure and taxation is to reduce regional inequalities by 40 per cent on average.

There were significant differences between measures applied in unitary and federal systems to correct the imbalances. In unitary states the redistribution takes place almost automatically, as high incomes attract high tax payments and low incomes high receipts of centrally funded services and transfer payments. In federations, intergovernmental grants and tax-sharing play a much bigger role, achieving large redistributive effects with a relatively small federal expenditure. Furthermore, public finance in economic unions plays a major role in cushioning short-term cyclical fluctuations. A large proportion of the loss of income in a region due to a fall in its external sales is automatically compensated for by lower tax revenues to the centre and higher social security benefits.

The implications of the MacDougall findings were that, if Europe is to integrate and move to an economic and monetary union, then public expenditure at European level will have to play a much more significant role in redistributing wealth between its richer and poorer members. This was partly recognized in 1988 by the decision to double the regional and social budgets by 1993 when the internal market will have been completed.

The decision of the European Council in 1988 to raise the ceiling for Community funding to 1.2 per cent of its GDP goes half-way towards the recommendation of the MacDougall Report for Community public expenditure to rise to 2–2½ per cent of GDP in the so called 'pre-federal integration period'. However, MacDougal recommended that as progress to full economic and monetary union is being made the federal budget should rise to between 5 per cent and 7 per cent of GDP. The target, more modest than in existing federations, is arrived at by leaving social security responsibilities in national hands. This would not, however, involve an increase in total public expenditure but merely a transfer of expenditure from national to Community levels.

From its higher income Community expenditure could be applied principally to reducing differences between regions in capital endowment and productivity. This would help the weaker regions to improve their performance and reduce their usually higher levels of unemployment. It could be done by the Community taking responsibility for a larger share than at present of regional aid and social funding dealing with employment problems. A possible candidate for the total transfer of national public expenditure to Community level could be development aid to third world countries. Another measure could be a limited budget equalization scheme, more modest but similar to those applied in existing federations like Canada, Germany, and the USA. This aims to bring the fiscal capacity of their constituent states to around the national average.

Were responsibility for defence of the Community to be transferred to it, as suggested in chapter 8, then paying for it would also become a Community responsibility. In such an event the proposed federal budget would rise to 7½–10 per cent and provide an additional dimension to the task of moderating inequalities in wealth within the union.

Where would the additional revenue come from? One possible

source is the newly reformed financial system, which relates contributions more closely to the levels of wealth of member states. As new responsibilities are transferred to the Community, contributions to finance them would have to be raised. There are other possible new sources of revenue, such as a share of corporate taxation, or a share of the social security contributions paid by individuals into a Community Unemployment Fund.

Another possible source could be a Community surtax on top of existing direct national taxes. Increases in revenue would, however, have to be matched by much greater accountability for its expenditure. The present institutional system of the Community lacks effective budgetary discipline. At present Council decisions, like those of the European Parliament, are influenced by the fact that neither institution is directly responsible to national electorates who raise the taxes to pay for them. Council members and European parliamentarians are much more likely to vote for higher Community expenditure if their own country would be a net beneficiary. If, as has long been the case, there are only a small minority of members who are net contributors, the majority will continue to press for large budget increases. That is why there has been a reluctance to transfer more budgetary powers to the European Parliament or abandon unanimity in the Council on these matters.

Yet, if the Community budget is to rise substantially as a share of GDP, institutional changes will have to be made to subject both revenue and expenditure to effective democratic control and make them directly accountable to the taxpayers. This might best be achieved if additional revenue were to come from the Community surtax on national taxation, as suggested above. If the surtax were clearly labelled as a European tax, individuals would become directly aware how much they pay in taxes to the Community. By acquiring budgetary powers and responsibilities equal to those of the Council, the directly elected Parliament would become much more accountable to the electorate for the financial management of the Community and for the taxes levied.

Chapter six

A people's Europe

What is it that could make people identify with Europe? What are the characteristics which distinguish this continent from others and which could command a greater allegiance than with peoples or countries outside it? Geographically we are a peninsula of the Asian land mass. Our populations are drawn from several families of nations, including Anglo-Saxons, Celts, Latins, and Slavs. Apart from many individual dialects, Europeans speak more than thirty distinct languages. As a result of past migrations from Europe to other continents links between Britain and the so-called white Commonwealth, for instance, have until now been closer than with the countries across the narrow English Channel. The same applies to the sense of kinship that France enjoys with French Canada, Spain with Latin America, or indeed most Europeans with their equivalent ethnic groups in America and elsewhere.

Prior to the emergence of the European Community, the growth of nationalism in the nineteenth century and the establishment of independent, sovereign nation states after the collapse of the German, Austro-Hungarian, Ottoman, and Russian empires in the twentieth century have stimulated rivalries and enmities between people of different nationalities. Within their own countries nation states have often sought to suppress ethnic minorities. To strengthen their internal unity, states have tended to centralize power at the expense of regional and local loyalties. Freedom of movement, of residence and the exercise of political and civil rights have been restricted to nationals within their own countries, thus isolating them from their neighbours. Passports and the requirement of visas for travel abroad, introduced during the twentieth century, have symbolized the separation of Europeans of different nationalities.

To enhance their separate identities, individual nation states have laid claim to the exclusive loyalty of their citizens. Thus European history, as taught in schools, is just a long litany of conflicts between fellow Europeans of different nationalities or allegiances. In these, the cause of one's own nation is almost always portrayed as just, unlike that of one's enemies. 'Our country, right or wrong', is the phrase that best summarizes the patriotism with which most Europeans have been brought up during this century.

It is easy enough to identify with the nation state. It has frontiers, national anthems, flags, postage stamps, taxes, passports, and a clearly recognizable national government. Most states are associated with a national language, literature, and history which induce a natural sense of belonging.

In addition, however, the people of the European countries have a great inheritance of distinct European values that have been indelibly shaped by a common cultural and historical heritage such as Greek thought, Roman law, Christianity and, more recently, the Renaissance with its immense influence upon architecture, literature, the arts, and music, the age of reason, the industrial revolution, imperialism, and social democracy. No more than a handful of countries in other continents enjoy similar standards of human rights and pluralist democracy and, where they do, their citizens either derive their ancestry from Europe or have adopted systems that follow the example of former European imperial masters. In this broad sense there is a distinct European identity. However, apart from a shared perception of common democratic values, only students of history or the arts are likely to recognize that we have a common European heritage.

The eminent Spanish author Salvador de Madariaga, who presided over the cultural commission of the first Congress of Europe in 1948, put the objective of promoting a common European identity in the following words in his foreword to a book by Kenneth Lindsay on *Towards a European Parliament*:

> Above all, we must love Europe; our Europe, sonorous with the roaring laughter of Rabelais, luminous with the smile of Erasmus, sparkling with the wit of Voltaire; in whose mental skies shine the fiery eyes of Dante, the clear eyes of Shakespeare, the serene eyes of Goethe, the tormented eyes of Dostoievski; this Europe to whom La Gioconda for ever smiles, where Moses and David spring to perennial life from Michelangelo's marble, and Bach's genius rises spontaneous to be caught in his intellectual geometry; where Hamlet seeks in thought the mystery of his inaction, and Faust seeks in action comfort for the void of his thought, where Don Juan seeks in women met the woman never found, and Don Quixote, spear in hand, gallops to force reality to rise above itself; this Europe where Newton and Leibniz measure the infinitesimal, and the Cathedrals, as Musset once wrote, pray on their knees in the robes of stone; where rivers, silver threads, link together strings of cities, jewels wrought in the

crystal of space by the chisel of time . . . this Europe must be born. And she will, when Spaniards will say 'our Chartres', Englishmen 'our Cracow', Italians 'our Copenhagen'; when Germans say 'our Bruges', and creep back horror-stricken at the idea of laying murderous hands on it. Then will Europe live, for then it will be that the Spirit that leads History will have uttered the creative words: 'Fiat Europe!'.

People in general need clear and tangible concepts in order to develop a sense of belonging. And that sense of identity is an indispensable factor in achieving and maintaining European unity. Jean Monnet recognized this when, at the end of his life, he said that if he had to begin again he would start with culture. With his wide experience of international co-operation he became increasingly convinced that problems blocking the path to political and economic union cannot be solved simply by compromise between national reservations. Most of the issues on monetary, taxation, trade and other matters are overshadowed by political considerations shaped by values which largely spring from distinct cultural attitudes and identities.

The Belgian Prime Minister, Leo Tindemans, similarly stressed the importance of the cultural dimension in his 1975 report on European Union, in the following words:

> The proposals for bringing Europe nearer to the citizen are directly in line with the deep-seated motivations behind the construction of Europe. They give it its social and human dimension. They attempt to restore to us at Union level that element of protection and control of our society which is progressively slipping from the grasp of State authority due to the nature of the problems and the international-isation of social life. They are essential to the success of our undertaking: the fact that our countries have a common destiny is not enough. This fact must also be seen to exist.

Rights and freedoms

What then are the factors that impinge directly on people's lives, and how have they been dealt with up to now during the process of European integration? First there are the human rights and fundamental liberties. These were enshrined in the European Convention for the Protection of Human Rights which formed part of the Statute of the Council of Europe set up in 1949. The European Court, established to ensure compliance with the convention, has jurisdiction binding on member states and there is access to it by individual citizens.

The right of free movement from one member state to another is a right guaranteed to all Community citizens. It is one of the fundamental principles of the treaties setting up the Community. This forbids all discrimination on grounds of nationality whether relating to employment, wages, social security, trade union rights, living and working conditions, housing, education, or vocational training. The only restrictions allowed on the free movement of workers are for justified reasons of public order, health, and safety, and for strictly defined employment in local or national public administration.

The rights include: equal pay for men and women, the right to work in the country of one's choice and to receive equal pay with workers native to that country, the right to buy and sell without being hindered by frontiers, the right to benefit from fair prices based on free competition and not on dominant market positions or monopolies, and finally the right to legal redress, across Community borders.

The equal treatment principle has been embodied in a whole series of regulations which abolish the need for a work permit, which guarantee most trade union rights, the right to education and job training, to social security payments and study grants. Enrolment and study fees must, for instance, be the same for all Community students.

Protection for women against discrimination on the grounds of their sex has been enshrined in Community law. These cover job descriptions, access to employment, training, promotion, working conditions, social security, the right of legal redress, and the protection of plaintiffs against retaliatory dismissal.

Legislation to protect women against discrimination has not been enough to stop it. The European Court of Justice has made many judgements requiring employers and others to fulfil their legal obligations. In 1981, for instance, the Court ruled against Lloyds Bank for refusing to give female employees under twenty-five the same pensions rights as other workers, on the grounds that an employer's pension contribution forms part of earnings. Compensation can be backdated, as was established by the Court in 1976 when a Belgian air hostess, whose pay was lower than that of male stewards, won her case.

Part-time workers are similarly protected. In a British case a lady working for a company producing women's clothes, who was earning 10 per cent per hour less than her full-time fellow workers, was judged to be subject to sexual discrimination. A similar judgement was given when a chain of Frankfurt shops refused to provide supplementary pensions for their part-time women workers.

There have been many cases of professional people wishing to practise in a country other than their own. Frequently, however, national legislation or professional rules have prevented them. In 1974, for instance, the Court judged that a Dutchman who studied law in Belgium was fully entitled to practise in that country. A few years later the Court ruled that a Belgian medical practitioner was entitled to set up a practice in Holland and a Belgian doctor of law to practise in France.

The problem was resolved in 1988 when the Council, acting to implement the Single European Act, decided that from the end of 1990 all professional people with a recognized national certificate, diploma or other professional qualification will have the right to set up anywhere within the Community. Some ten million people within the Community are affected, including teachers, librarians, lawyers, bankers, accountants, members of the medical professions, engineers, builders, foresters, etc. The new principle is that any person qualified for a particular profession in one member state will be free to practise in any of the other eleven.

The only qualification to this full freedom of establishment is the right of the host state to require a test to be taken for all those professions which require a knowledge of domestic law. This could apply to lawyers, insurers, patent agents, etc. For all other professions where there could be some divergences in their training in different countries, immigrating professionals may be required to undergo a limited probationary period before being given full freedom to practise in the host state.

Community law states that migrants from another member state must be treated like nationals of the host country. This applies as much to employees as to their dependants. There have been several examples of immigrant workers who gained Court judgements in their favour. There was the case of a seriously disabled son of an Italian who was refused welfare payments in France on grounds of his nationality. The dependent mother of another Italian worker, living in Belgium, obtained income payable to retired Belgians. There have been Britons and Dutch, without visible means of support, who have received Belgian benefits the same as those guaranteed to their own nationals. Interest-free loans payable to new parents under regional legislation in the state of Baden-Württemberg were judged to be equally applicable to an Italian couple working in Stuttgart.

All disputes concerning the rights of individuals under Community law are subject to the final and binding rulings of the European Court of Justice. Access to it is not limited to European Community institutions and to member states. Many of the Court's judgements stem from individuals invoking Community laws in their national courts, even in cases where a member state has failed fully to adapt its legislation to that laid down by the Community. Judges may consult the European Court of Justice for its ruling. In cases where a judicial decision cannot be appealed to a higher national court, the right of access to the European Court is guaranteed.

Two further improvements to protect the rights of individuals suggest themselves. A European Equal Opportunities Commission might be given the task of looking into cases of discrimination between citizens of different Community countries and, where appropriate, submit these for adjudication to the European Court of Justice. The second proposal would be to establish an office of a European Ombudsman to look into all cases of maladministration within Community institutions. Submissions might best be routed via members of the European Parliament. Both of these proposals would lessen the present costs and shorten procedures for citizens seeking to secure their European rights.

Europeans gained some of their democratic rights within the Community with the institution in 1979 of direct elections to the European Parliament, which now take place every five years. Although parliamentary powers are still rather limited, citizens can make representations to the Parliament individually or in groups. It can either act as a mediator or make direct representations to member states and to the European Commission.

Consumers

But it is as consumers that European integration has had a rapid and major impact on the daily lives of people. The abolition of customs barriers widened the choice of goods and services, and this will increase substantially. Prices are likely to become even more competitive once non-tariff barriers are eliminated and the single market becomes fully established after 1992.

A European consumer policy was first established when the October 1972 Summit ruled that improvement in the quality of life was the first priority of economic development. To implement it a directorate-general for the environment and consumer protection was set up within the Commission. A Consumers' Consultative Committee was given the task of providing a forum for consumer associations to consult with each other and with Community institutions, and the Community adopted several programmes for consumers. These were designed to safeguard health and safety, protect consumers' economic interests, give value for money, and guarantee the right to redress or damages.

Health and safety protection has for long been a national concern. But differing national standards and technical regulations have often impeded the free flow of goods across frontiers. This problem was first overcome by a seminal judgement of the European Court of Justice in 1979, in the 'Cassis de Dijon' case, which established the principle that a product legally made and sold in one country should be admitted to the market of every other member state. This principle has been accepted as a basis for the completion of the single internal market.

Consumers are also protected through a wide range of Community directives covering food products and their purity. Regulations govern the composition, manufacture, and naming of honeys, jams, marmalades, fruit juices, mineral waters, tinned milk, and cocoa and coffee products. Rules are also laid down for the presentation, labelling, and packaging of foodstuffs. Other goods subjected to regulations for consumer protection include cosmetics, textiles, pharmaceuticals, dangerous substances, and manufactured goods such as cars and tractors.

Since 1984 member states have been obliged to inform the Commission and other member states of any serious accidents requiring urgent measures to protect the health and safety of consumers and prevent future accidents. This is particularly relevant to children's toys, which may contain lead, for instance, or other dangerous products. To this end the Commission publishes guides on accident prevention.

Protection against dishonest and improper trading practices is another area of Community concern. Directives have been issued on misleading advertising, door-to-door sales, manufacturer's responsibility for damage caused by a defective product, on consumer credit, the importation of counterfeit products, and on redress available to consumers.

Tourism

Travel and tourism within Europe has become big business. Some 20 per cent of people who take holidays, go to another Community country. Most travel by road, others by rail, air, or on water. Tourism represents some $5\frac{1}{2}$ per cent of the Community's GDP and 8 per cent of private consumption. It provides the equivalent of 5.5 million full-time jobs and, being a major growth area, it can make an important contribution to creating new jobs and developing backward regions.

Yet amongst the most irritating experiences of tourism across Community borders are long delays whilst passports are checked and travellers questioned by customs officers in what is supposed to be a customs-free Community. Things have improved in recent years, but there is still much to be done in the run-up to 1992. The aim is ultimately to remove all police, tax, and customs checks at borders.

Emergency medical care, on the same conditions as that provided to their own nationals, is now available to all Community citizens. A European emergency health card has been devised, which contains medical information in all languages necessary for the safety of such travellers as diabetics or those with a heart condition. So is access to legal aid to those visiting another Community country.

Duty free allowances have been substantially increased and

insurance companies must now provide third party cover for motorists and their families travelling to other Community countries. Finally a Community driving licence has been introduced and all driving licences issued by member states must now conform to the Community model.

Community financial aid plays an important role in expanding tourism in member countries. Between 1980 and 1983 the European Investment Bank gave low-interest loans totalling Ecu 350 million (£235 million) for more than 1,000 tourist projects. Amongst the most notable have been loans to restore and maintain important cultural monuments such as the Doge's Palace in Venice and the Parthenon in Athens. Grants from the European Regional Development Fund totalling Ecu 326 million (£220 million) during the same period have also aided some 660 tourist projects, including holiday villages, pleasure harbours, ski lifts, hotels, sport and conference centres, bathing resorts, museums, and archaeological sites.

Finally the Community is directly concerned with improving the working conditions for those engaged in the tourist industry. Studies have been financed to examine employment in hotels, restaurants, and cafés, and to standardize computer vocabularies and access to data banks for hotel reservation systems. Community directives lay down that all jobs in the tourist industry, including interpreters, couriers, and guides can be practised by Community citizens in any country of their choice. Help is available for vocational training abroad, particularly important for language practice.

Education

The whole issue of education plays a central role in the Community's strategy to train people for work outside their own country. But the principal role of the Community's education policy is to promote better mutual understanding and the growth of a European consciousness.

Many people believe that the biggest barrier to unity is the fact that Europeans speak so many languages. True, but so do the polyglot citizens of the Soviet Union and India. The latter in particular offers a good example to Europe. The Indian Union's two official languages are Hindi and English. The constitution also recognizes sixteen main languages used for official purposes within individual states. All India Radio broadcasts in fifty-one languages and eighty-two tribal dialects. Of course there is a natural desire to ensure that the use of one's own language is not diminished and that its cultural heritage, in the form of literature, does not atrophy. That is certainly not the aim or intention of European integration.

There is, however, the problem of the high cost of translations and interpretation within Community institutions. With twelve member states there are nine official languages and under existing rules all documents have to appear in them. Simultaneous interpretation into all the languages has also to be provided for most meetings. The problem will not become easier if the Community is further enlarged. Turkey has already applied and the accession of some further Scandinavian countries is also possible.

In the Council of Europe, with twenty-two member countries, the accepted official languages are English and French. To adopt this practice within the Community institutions may not be easy, but it has been suggested that, in fairness to the others, people should not use their own mother tongue. This would mean that the French would have to use English and the British, French. Whatever the wishes of those anxious to preserve their own tongues, the trend in Europe and throughout the world, seems to be towards the universal use of English for international communication.

Nevertheless the Community is committed to preserving multilingualism as a feature of its cultural richness. To do this it encourages language teaching for which guidance and financial help is given. Schools are recommended to teach not less than two other languages. Help is also given for the translation of major literary works originally written in minority languages.

Beyond the knowledge of foreign languages, a most important contribution to mutual understanding and the building of a common European consciousness lies in the teaching of European history. In virtually every country the history taught in its schools has a hoary accumulation of subjective national bias, often hostile to its neighbours, that should now be weeded out. Over a period, national history curricula ought to be redesigned to ensure that national history is taught within the context of its wider European and world framework.

Exchanges

To reduce ignorance of each other's countries, languages, and cultures more is necessary than just better education in schools. By far the best way to get to know one's neighbours is to visit each other. And here organized exchanges between people can play a vital role, particularly when young people go to stay with a family in another country.

Many motorists are struck by the Council of Europe signposts at the entry to towns and villages which announce their twinning with other European places. Although such twinnings have often seemed to be confined to bilateral junketings of the respective Mayors and the chief executives, many local authorities have developed links well beyond the official exchange of visits and information. These include parallel twinning arrangements between local schools, trades councils, and voluntary bodies concerned with sport and leisure activities. Exchange visits, joint events, and holidays involving people in the twinned localities, particularly if well covered in the local press, can contribute effectively to mutual understanding and the reduction of narrow-minded parochialism.

But it is exchanges between young people that are likely to make the biggest long-term impact. The best illustration has been the intensive and well-financed programme of bilateral youth exchanges between France and Germany which started in the 1950s. Millions of French and German young people have participated in the well-designed programmes aimed at removing the traditional rivalry and hostility that characterized their countries' relations over the centuries. The results have been most impressive. The hostility and suspicion, that can still be found amongst those who, as adults, lived through the last war, have totally disappeared amongst the younger generations.

To this end the Community has now promoted a programme open to all young Europeans, called YES (Youth Exchange Scheme). The project, which started in 1988 with a budget of Ecu 30 million (£20 million) for the first three years, aims to promote exchanges for some 80,000 young people between the ages of fifteen and twenty-five, who will spend at least one week in another Community country, having been first prepared through suitable instruction about the economic, social, and cultural aspects of the country to be visited. It is to be hoped that the scheme will be much extended, with adequate financial resources to match the excellent results achieved by the Franco-German experience.

Another major programme, ERASMUS (European Community Action Scheme for the Mobility of University Students), involves some 3,600 higher education establishments, with some 6 million students. It provides an opportunity for some of these students to do part of their studies in a university or higher education institute in another Community state.

Initially allocated Ecu 85 million (£57 million) for the first three years of its operation up to 1990, ERASMUS has several elements. Participating educational institutions conclude agreements for student and teacher exchanges and draw up joint teaching programmes. Grants are available for students to spend at least one term abroad. The period of study must be recognized by the original university through the development of a European course credit transfer system.

Another contribution to education is the COMETT programme, described in chapter 4. This stands for the programme of 'the Community in education and training for technology'. The money allocated for its first operational phase from 1987 to 1989 was Ecu 45 million (£30 million). It has financed university–industry training partnerships at universities, which have provided transnational placements in industry for students, and fellowships for executives from industry.

A common identity

Building a European consciousness must, however, extend well beyond the education of our young. It needs to permeate everyday concerns and interests of Community citizens, including sport, cultural pursuits, and television. In June 1984, the European Council set up an Ad Hoc Committee for a People's Europe. It was asked to suggest ways of strengthening the identity and improving the image of the Community. Under the chairmanship of Pietro Addonino, the committee submitted two reports which were approved by the heads of governments (EC Commission 1985a).

Amongst its many proposals it recommended the introduction and development of a Community dimension to sport. As a consequence the Community now sponsors cycling tours and European tennis, football, swimming, and other sport championships. A 'Sail for Europe' Association has organized round the world cruises and Tour de France yacht races crewed by young sailors drawn from several member countries. European driving rallies and 'walks for Europe' have also taken place.

With millions of people following sporting events, the promotion of European sporting events has made an important contribution to mutual understanding, despite the deplorable examples of football hooliganism that have marred some events. Indeed, the shame they have generated nationally has strengthened ties through efforts to make amends. There were, for instance, significant gestures of reconciliation made through exchange visits of goodwill between the English and Italians following the tragic loss of Italian lives after the Heysel Stadium football riot in Belgium.

One way of promoting the European sporting dimension is to have the competitors of the twelve member countries wear a Community symbol at future Olympic Games. In the Los Angeles Games in 1984, for example, athletes of the twelve countries won 188 medals which was more than the 174 won by the Americans. Although there cannot be a single team of Community competitors until we have a full European Union, wearing a common symbol is certainly a useful first step towards it.

The creation of a European cultural area is another desirable objective. The aim is the free circulation of cultural goods and services. This covers the free movement of works of art, with business sponsorship being encouraged to mount major European exhibitions and shows. Better living and working conditions for artists as well as more information about cultural Europe are other objectives. Promotion of cultural activities in the regions is helped by Community grants and by the designation of 'European Cities of Culture'. The sponsorship of the European Symphony and Chamber Youth Orchestras has led to the creation of ensembles of high professional competence that have delighted audiences throughout the world.

The most important role in promoting a European consciousness is that of the media, with television obviously playing a decisive part. With the proliferation of television satellites, programmes will be beamed simultaneously into homes throughout Europe. Technological developments are taking place to establish one television market with a single European television standard. By 1992 there may be up to 200 TV channels available in Europe. If these are not to be dominated by the Americans, the Community must ensure the establishment of multinational and multilingual European television programmes and stations. With suitable technological development it should soon be possible to provide satellite television broadcasts beamed simultaneously in different languages according to the viewers' choice.

The financing, production, and distribution of such broadcasts is already the subject of the Community's MEDIA programme. In the field of fiction series for TV, the MEDIA programme is helping to finance the Geneva-Europe prize for scripts. A European Group of Cinema and Audio-Visual Financiers was established in 1987 to help finance European co-productions. The Community hopes to assist the setting up of a European co-operative for the distribution of low-budget films.

The 1988 European Cinema and Television Year, jointly organized by the European Community and the Council of Europe, set out to draw the attention of the public – and of professional and political circles – to film and television as a means of promoting Europe's originality, identity, and creative potential. It included symposia on European co-productions and co-distribution, as well as on pirating of audio-visual works. Several European film prizes will in future be awarded.

Symbols of unity

Symbols can play an important part in encouraging people to identify with the European Community. The adoption in 1986 of the old Council of Europe flag, consisting of a circle of twelve gold stars on a blue background, has helped. So could increasing use of the European anthem – the prelude of the 'Ode to Joy' from Beethoven's Ninth Symphony. Every 9th of May is now celebrated as Europe Day, commemorating the 1950 Schuman Declaration which gave birth to the Community?

The Community now also has a common passport, even if it did take some ten years of argument to agree on its colour and format. Useful though this may be to identify European citizens beyond Community borders, do we really want a passport to cross what are soon to be non-existent frontiers within the Community? Increasingly people find it necessary to carry some form of identity card, even if having and carrying them is not compulsory in every country. Nowadays many already carry driving licences, credit cards, and travel passes. Would it not be preferable if every European citizen were issued with a common identity card with a photograph, which they could use instead of a passport for travel within the Community?

The adoption of a single European currency, discussed in chapter 3 will naturally have a most significant impact on people's identification with the Community, as would, though less favourably, a European tax as suggested in chapter 5. Also highly effective would be the setting up of a genuine European government.

Common citizenship

What we need above all, however, is a common European citizenship, enshrined in law and with clearly defined rights. Present European Community law does not embrace all the rights and duties normally associated with citizenship of a democratic state. The formal creation of a European Community citizenship would, however, give a strong political boost to the development of a European identity. The Draft Treaty for European Union, adopted by the European Parliament in 1984, expressed this in the following phrase in article 3: 'The citizens of the member states shall *ipso facto* be citizens of the Union.'

Such a declaration would have to be accompanied by the setting out of a number of basic rights. These would include those already available, such as protection outside the Community, as asked for in the European passport, the right to live in freedom within the law, as laid down in the European Convention for the Protection of Human Rights, and the right to move, live, and work freely throughout the Community.

In one area, however, the democratic rights of European citizens need to be extended. They already have the right to vote in European parliamentary elections, though fair representation within the Parliament still awaits agreement on a common electoral system. Under the present British electoral system voters are denied fair representation in the European Parliament which would correspond to the votes actually cast for candidates of different political parties. Furthermore, the absence of proportional representation in Britain, practised throughout the rest of the Community, causes a major distortion in the distribution of seats amongst all the European political party groups in the Parliament.

If, however, Europeans are free to live under the law anywhere within the Community, and are obliged to pay taxes locally or nationally, then surely they should be given all the democratic rights which accompany such freedoms and duties. The demand for no taxation without representation is as relevant within the Community as it was in the American colonies that fought to create their own union. Representation must give all European citizens the right to vote and offer themselves as candidates in local, regional, national, and European elections, irrespective of the country in which they live.

There is little doubt that the emergence of the European Community and its growing integration has eroded some of the shackles and restraints which nation states have imposed on their citizens. There is also evidence that people are becoming more conscious of a common European identity and that this need not conflict with continuing national, regional or local loyalties. Regular opinion polls conducted throughout the Community, referred to in chapter 10, show a growing understanding that European unity does not involve the sacrifice of national cultural identity. Indeed, in the face of challenges from the super-powers, European Union is increasingly recognized as the best guarantee for the preservation of Europe's most precious characteristic and asset – its cultural diversity. But it has to be a union founded on federal principles if its diverse cultural riches and the plurality of people's loyalties are to be protected. The nature of such a federal union is the subject of the next chapter.

Chapter seven

A federal democracy

As a result of the technological revolution ever more rapid change has become the norm. Since the last world war modern industrial society has become much more complex and its management has led to a massive increase of government involvement in people's daily lives. Economic management, physical planning and environmental control, transport and communications, and social, health, and welfare provisions are all relatively new concerns of government. They require a vast and complex machinery to administer. And so in modern industrial countries public sector expenditure accounts for nearly half of their gross national product. Most of these new responsibilities and powers have gone to national governments and central administrations.

This centralization leads to functions and resources being accumulated in relatively small geographic locations, usually within easy reach of metropolitan areas especially around national capital cities. These dominate the rest of the country, relegating vast parts to a peripheral and subsidiary role. Such concentration is not confined to government functions but inevitably extends to commerce and industry, to culture and centres of excellence, all of which want to be close to where power and money reside.

Within the European Community such concentration of functions and resources has occurred in the triangle between London, Paris, and the Ruhr. Cities like Athens, Milan, and Naples have grown in all directions attracting people, wealth, and activities away from the countryside and the smaller towns and villages. The trend has had serious consequences.

The peripheral areas remain underdeveloped, culturally deprived, and increasingly depopulated. The metropolitan conurbations, congested and expensive, have turned into maelstroms of feverish activity. City centres have become increasingly dehumanized, centres where mental illness, drugs and crime have escalated.

Many local communities have lost their sense of identity. With decisions about their lives taken, usually far away, by faceless bureaucracies, people have become increasingly alienated from their governments. Democratic accountability of national governments to their citizens through elected representatives has become tenuous. Parliaments find it ever more difficult to check the activities of burgeoning administrations. Representative democracy, meant to give ordinary citizens a say over their lives, is becoming discredited through growing cynicism about politicians. A sense of community has been replaced by a general feeling of 'them and us' as the gap between government and governed has alarmingly widened.

One consequence has been the proliferation of single issue politics, campaigns, and demonstrations. Traditional methods of democratic control through elected representatives have been increasingly marginalized. Representative democracy is being undermined and questioned as people demand direct participation in the decision-making process.

In most of the modern industrialized countries existing institutions are failing to respond to the needs and demands of ordinary citizens. Rapid change in our technological society and the massive increase in governmental responsibilities clearly require that our institutions adapt to the new circumstances if democracy is to survive. What is needed in particular is much greater flexibility and the diffusion of over-centralized powers.

Some European countries have managed to avoid the worst features of alienation and the discredit of existing democratic processes. Switzerland, for instance, provides a remarkable contrast. People in their local communities feel they belong and have a clear say over most decisions which affect them, be it at local, regional, or national level. Both direct and representative democracy operate alongside each other. Frequent referenda are used as a guide for elected representatives governing villages, towns, cantons, and the whole Swiss Confederation.

Plebiscites and referenda, discredited in Nazi times, have no such place in the German Federal Republic. Yet the sense of community and a strong attachment to democratic processes is characteristic of German society. Villages and towns are well administered by elected representatives and people feel very much part of their local communities. Regional governments, established after the war and exercised at Laender level, have extensive responsibilities and powers under the control of their state parliaments. The federal government is subject to wide constitutional checks and balances. As a reaction and revulsion against the Nazi era, post-war Germany has become the most stable and probably the strongest bastion of representative democracy in Europe.

The federal system

What distinguishes Germany and Switzerland from other western European states is that they are both federations. Within them power is distributed between the different levels of government. The distribution is based on the principle of subsidiarity according to which all governmental decisions are taken at the lowest level possible and closest to the citizen. Each tier of government is furthermore democratically accountable to representative parliaments or assemblies elected directly by the public. The powers of the lower tiers of government are constitutionally guaranteed against their encroachment by the higher levels. Whilst each tier enjoys autonomy in the functions and responsibilities allocated to it, many powers are shared and co-ordinated. Disputes are usually resolved by reference to a Federal Tribunal, in Switzerland, and to the Federal Constitutional Court in Germany.

Professor Maurice Vile defined federalism as a system of government in which central, regional, and local authorities are linked in a mutually interdependent political relationship; in this system a balance is maintained such that neither level of government becomes dominant to the extent that it can dictate the decisions of the others, but each can influence, bargain with, and persuade the others (Vile 1973).

With the massive increase of governmental functions and responsibilities, the advantages of their diffusion have been recognized in many European countries. Devolution of powers from the centre has taken place in Italy, largely as a reaction against the overcentralized state under fascist rule. The state has been territorially decentralized to grant substantial local autonomy not only to provincial and communal councils but also to an intermediate tier of regional government.

Belgium has a strong local government tradition, with its existence guaranteed by the constitution. There are two tiers of local government exercising a general competence under the supervision of the national government. The linguistic divisions between Flemish and French speaking areas have recently led to the federal division of the country into three autonomous self-governing regions.

The Netherlands, although a unitary state, has a well-established system of local government consisting of eleven provinces and 842 municipalities, each with elected councils, to which in recent years the national government has consciously transferred powers previously centrally exercised.

Decentralization has also taken place in Denmark and France. The latest French reform has created directly elected regional councils with new powers to levy their own taxes, employ staff, and administer their own projects. Since the re-establishment of democracy in Spain, the highly centralized state has been transformed into a federation of seventeen regions, each with its flag, capital, government, and parliament. Indeed the trend, practically throughout western Europe, has been decentralization with a steady shift of powers from central to subnational levels of government.

Britain alone is moving against this trend. Pressure for regional devolution, be it to Scotland, Wales, or the other regions of England, is being strongly resisted. Democratically elected metropolitan authorities for London and other major conurbations have been abolished. Local government is being emasculated, with its powers increasingly concentrated at the centre where national ministers and their civil servants have the final say. In the absence of a written constitution the status of local government has in the past relied on convention, with its legitimacy as a proper part of the democratic system dependent on consensus politics. Under the Thatcher administration terms such as consensus and co-operation are no longer fashionable and the principle that Westminster knows best is its dominant characteristic.

The European dimension

Against this background of a general diffusion of powers from the centre to regional and local tiers in most European countries, except for Britain, a new dimension to the issue of the distribution of powers has arisen with the creation of the European Community. As the story of its evolution, recounted in chapter 2, has demonstrated, the Community's institutions are continually evolving as they acquire new responsibilities. Each stage in its evolution from the very first European Coal and Steel Community has been seen as yet another step in what Robert Schuman in 1950 described as, 'laying the foundations of a European federation', referred to by others as the European Union.

What is often not realized by protagonists of federal devolution within nation states is that the federation of such states into larger entities is merely the other side of the same coin. It is part of a coherent system concerned with the whole range of interdependent levels of government, each democratically accountable to its own elected representative councils, assemblies, or parliaments with constitutionally guaranteed powers. Thus the attempt to federate Europe can be seen as the response to the changing nature of society, brought about by its growing interdependence and complexity in the wake of the technological revolution, which is echoed by demands for devolution of powers within nation states towards democratically accountable and autonomous regional and local authorities.

Semantic arguments about the description to be given to the process of European integration are in themselves not very important. Its substance is. As Edward Heath, in the inaugural Lothian Memorial Lecture in November 1987 put it: 'the Community was created by the founding fathers as an institution *sui generis*'. He did not believe that it was very productive to spend time arguing about federalism and its many different definitions. The final form of the Community's political organization will be *sui generis*, and he urged that one should instead concentrate on making the Community a success in all its different forms (Heath 1988).

Edward Heath's view is understandable when expressed in Britain where federalism has for many people long been a dirty word. The aversion is surprising because federal ideas and their practice play a distinct part in the British political tradition. Towards the end of the First World War, for instance, serious consideration was given by the British government to a scheme of Irish home rule which would fit in with a federal plan designed to facilitate Home Rule all round in the United Kingdom. It surfaced more recently during the devolution debates in the mid-1970s and is still one of the options considered for the solution of the Irish problem.

As the Empire was being transformed into a Commonwealth, the British successfully fathered federations all over the world, including Australia, Canada, India, Nigeria, and Malaysia, and somewhat less successfully in Rhodesia and the West Indies. Federal Union, founded in Britain and backed by leading politicians and academics at the outbreak of the Second World War, played a seminal role in the development of plans and ideas that led to the creation of the European Community. And the Anglo-French Union proposed by Churchill and his government in June 1940 would have created a federation.

British hostility to the federal idea was fomented by establishment figures who opposed British participation in the building of the European Community after the Second World War. Since Britain joined the Community, those who want to resist the development of its institutions have played on the belief that British cultural values would be submerged within an alien continental European tradition.

The fear that we would all become foreigners is a major public misconception of federalism in its application to European unity. In a recent speech to the European Parliament, the Queen of The Netherlands pointed out that it is a common mistake to regard the political development of the European Community as a 'development comparable to the evolution of a nation state'. Social homogeneity and cultural standardization are not part of the Community's purpose. On the contrary the whole history of European integration since the 1950s clearly demonstrates that the aim of the Community is to preserve and enhance Europe's social and cultural diversity. Indeed the very essence of federalism is a federal constitution that safeguards the autonomy and integrity of its component states. This is to prevent the cultural identities of individual countries being subsumed, as they surely would, were they to merge into a super-state without constitutional guarantees.

Part of the confusion is generated by the uncertainty about the form a future European federation might take. Many people imagine that advocates of the United States of Europe wish to replicate the system operated within the USA. Yet there are many different federal systems in existence in other parts of the world, each with its own distinct structure, adapted to the needs and wishes of its founders. Thus the USA has a presidential system under which the executive is separate from the legislature. Canada retains the British monarch as the head of state. Its government consists of a prime minister and cabinet chosen, as in Britain, from the House of Commons. The members of the upper chamber, the senate, are appointed like members of the House of Lords by the monarch, through his representative, the Governor-General. Unlike the British system, however, the two chambers enjoy equal powers. The provinces have single chamber legislatures from which its governments are chosen.

Australia has a similar federal system, but their senate is directly elected. Their provincial territories, each operating under separate constitutions, have two chamber legislatures, except for Queensland.

The Soviet Union is also a federation composed of fifteen sovereign republics each with its own constitution. Until recently, however, the Soviet Union has been one of the most centralized states with most decisions handed down by the Supreme Soviet representing the government of the federation. This in turn was controlled by the Politbureau of the Communist Party.

The Indian federation resembles those of Canada and Australia, though its organization has been adapted to take account of the wide diversity of ethnic character, language, and religion of its huge and mainly rural population.

The most decentralized federation is Switzerland, where the bulk of governmental powers is exercised by its component cantons, each with their own constitution and laws, and an executive drawn from an elected legislature. Sovereignty resides in the twenty-three cantons and the federal government exercises only those powers which have been vested in it by the constitution of the federation, drawn up by the cantons. Changes in the constitution require approval by a majority of all federal voters in a referendum, and a majority of voters in a majority of cantons.

The diversity of federal systems stems from the historical origins and distinctive cultural backgrounds of each federation and none can be regarded as the correct model for the European Community to follow. It is in this sense that Edward Heath was right to claim that Europe's political organization will be *sui generis*, but there is little doubt that its development will be on federal lines.

The European Community has many federal features already. Its constitution consists of the treaties which set it up and the many institutional reforms introduced during its existence. The latest amongst them is the Single European Act. The guarantor and interpreter of the constitution is the European Court of Justice whose judgements are binding on all member states as well as on its citizens. The Community's Council of Ministers has the power to pass laws that override national legislation and are binding on all. It has a directly elected Parliament with supervisory powers over the European Commission, the governing organ of the Community; it has the final say over the Community's budget and, increasingly, it participates in the legislative process.

Nevertheless the Community's institutions are still some distance from providing a European government with real democratic accountability and real, if limited powers, which would transform the Community into a federation or union, to the creation of which member countries have repeatedly declared they are committed. What further changes would then be required for the objective to be achieved? First there is need for the Community's competences to be extended to defence and foreign policy – issues covered in the next two chapters. But even with its present responsibilities a review of the structure, functions, and powers of each institution will illustrate its strengths and weaknesses, and indicate where reform could make it more effective.

The Commission

The Commission is the executive organ of the Community. Its members, although appointed by national governments, are under no obligations to them, and their loyalty, expressed in an oath on taking office, is pledged to the Community alone. At present the Commission consists of seventeen members, two each from the five larger states and one each from the seven smaller countries. They are appointed by their national governments for four-year terms which are renewable. The President of the Commission is appointed for renewable two year terms by all the member governments jointly. Each commissioner is allocated an area of responsibility, usually proposed by the President at the start of his term. Decisions within the Commission are taken in private and, if necessary, by simple majority vote.

The functions of the Commission are summarized as being those of initiative, supervision, and implementation. It has the specific right to propose legislation to the Council, to implement the Council's decisions and generally to see that the legislation and other provisions laid down by the treaties are carried out. Under its direct control is a staff of

European civil servants who, like the Commissioners, owe allegiance to the Community alone, even though leading officials are usually drawn from national civil services.

The Commission, whose members are mostly politicians, represents the governing cabinet, though its President cannot be compared to a prime minister. He neither selects nor decides on the functions of his fellow commissioners. He cannot dismiss them either. The Commission, as a whole, is answerable to the European Parliament who can censure and dismiss it, a power never yet exercised.

The European Parliament, in its Draft Treaty for European Union, adopted in February 1984, proposed only small changes. It recommended that the Commission's term of office should start within six months following the election of the Parliament. As the latter is elected for five year terms, the Commission's term would thus be extended. The principal change would give the President of the Commission the right to select his own fellow commissioners after consulting the European Council. The Commission would then submit its programme to the Parliament and take office after its investiture by the Parliament. It would remain in office until the investiture of a new Commission.

The importance of these reforms lies in two aspects. The Commission would become much more directly accountable to the European Parliament. The President's powers of appointment and, presumably, the right to allocate functions to his fellow commissioners would enhance his powers and status. To the public at large, however, the Commission would continue to present its current shadowy and rather faceless image.

From time to time, proposals have been put forward by European statesmen for the election of a President of the European Union to enhance its public image and the democratic legitimacy of its government. More recently the European Parliament has proposed that the President of the Commission should be elected by the Parliament, on a nomination submitted by the European Council, before the other members of the Commission are appointed. This should take place immediately following each parliamentary election with a five-year term of office for the Commission to coincide with the Parliament's own term. Another possible way of achieving this objective would be through the direct election of the President of the Commission by universal suffrage, without necessarily increasing his powers. This would, at one stroke, focus public attention on the Union and raise public perception of the Commission to the level comparable to that of, say, the French presidency. If his election were held at the same time as those of the European Parliament, it would no doubt increase public participation in European elections from their currently low levels. In line with the American example a vice-president, elected on the same ticket, could be the President of the Parliament.

The Council

Whilst the Commission represents the general European interest, the Council of Ministers brings to bear the interests of the member states on the decision-making process. The Council consists of representatives from each of the member states with its meetings attended by at least one commissioner. The membership of the Council is, however, constantly changing, depending on the subject under discussion. Thus finance ministers deal with the budget, agricultural ministers with the CAP, and industrial ministers with matters related to industry. Foreign Ministers meet at least once a month in a General Affairs Council which, apart from foreign affairs, co-ordinates the work of the specialist Councils.

The principal legislature in the Community is the Council, to whom proposals for new laws, known as directives or regulations, are submitted by the Commission. Subject to opinions which have to be sought from the European Parliament, and often from the Economic and Social Committee, it is the Council that enacts the legislation. Contrary to practice in most parliamentary democracies, the Council debates and enacts the laws behind closed doors.

Under the Treaty most decisions are supposed to be reached by qualified majority (now fifty-four votes out of seventy-six). Only a limited range of issues of major importance require unanimous agreement. The so-called Luxembourg compromise, reached in 1966, led to the practical suspension of all majority voting. If unanimity was not obtainable, issues were either dropped or allowed to lie on the table, often for years on end. The effect was to stultify progress and subordinate Community interests to those of individual member states.

For years many urgent reforms could not be effected. Where decisions were taken they tended to be of the lowest common denominator. Compromises reflected bargains between individual states where one government might give way on issues on which it was not convinced in exchange for concessions on often quite unrelated matters. This process of 'log-rolling' may have satisfied some national interests but, inevitably, at the expense of the common good. The most notorious example of this practice has been in the handling of the Common Agricultural Policy, where log-rolling led to massive and costly overproduction, eating up for years up to three-quarters of the Community budget.

An examination of most criticisms levelled at the European Community over the years shows that responsibility for failure to make progress, for botched decisions, for delay and procrastination, and even for mismanagement resulting from flawed legislation lies with national governments and their representatives in the Community institutions. The habit of taking decisions only by unanimous agreement bred an attitude of mind that always put the national and even local parochial interest before that of the Community. On many occasions junior national civil servants vetoed consideration of minor legislative changes on the grounds that their government or minister would not approve.

Finally feeling grew that to end the stagnation to meet the challenges facing it in the world at large, majority voting would have to return. And so the Treaty was amended by the Single European Act to reduce substantially issues on which unanimous agreement was required. On other issues, for which the treaties so provide, if agreement could not be reached, majority voting would actually be applied.

Since a proposal can be blocked by twenty-three votes out of seventy-six, only three large states acting together, or two large states with one small one (excepting Luxembourg) can block adoption. It would require at least five of the smaller states (with five votes each or less) to do so. The remarkable progress actually achieved towards the enactment of the nearly 300 legislative proposals needed to create the single market is the best evidence of the benefits of abandoning the principle of unanimity. The mere threat of being outvoted is often quite enough to push governments towards compromise.

The Council operates under a rotating presidency. Member states take turns for six month periods and its representatives chair Council meetings. The function of the presidency should be to steer the Council towards agreement on as many as possible of the issues presented by the Commission. During the term of each presidency a summit meeting is held of Heads of Governments, called the European Council. Foreign Ministers are designated Presidents of the Council during their country's term of presidency.

The work of the Council is prepared and assisted by large national delegations based in Brussels, headed by Permanent Representatives with a status and rank of senior ambassadors. The committee of permanent representatives, called COREPER meets weekly and tries to reach agreement on proposals submitted by the Commission. Those agreed are usually adopted by the appropriate Council without further debate. Controversial issues are left to the Councils to resolve. The final arbiter in cases where the Council has been unable to reach agreement is the summit meeting of the European Council.

Sir Michael Butler, a former British Permanent Representative, in his book *Europe: More than a Continent*, published in 1986, summarized the functions of the Council in the following terms: 'In one sense, COREPER and the Council together are a forum for a permanent negotiation between member governments on a wide range of issues simultaneously. In another, they are the legislature of the Community. In a third, they are the senior board of directors taking many of the day to day decisions on its policies' (Butler 1986).

The European Parliament's Draft Treaty for European Union does not envisage major changes to the Council. It recommends that each country's representatives should be led by a minister who is permanently and specifically responsible for Union affairs. The substantive changes deal with legislation. Where, under the Draft Treaty, the Union has exclusive competence or concurrent powers with member states, absolute or qualified majority voting would apply. Some policy areas are reserved for 'co-operation', where decisions would require unanimous agreement.

During the long period between 1966 and 1985, when most decisions by the Council depended on unanimous agreement or consensus, the originally envisaged balance of power between Community institutions had become distorted. The Council became the dominant institution with the Commission increasingly relegated to the function of civil servants, even though it retained the exclusive right to propose legislation. It is not surprising, therefore, that European issues and concerns were subordinated to national interests and the Community slowly ground to a halt. The adoption of the Single European Act, with majority voting on most issues covered by it, enables the distribution of powers between Community institutions to be brought back into balance.

The day-to-day management and conduct of Community affairs will increasingly revert to the Commission. The question arises, however, whether the rotating presidency of the Council is really the most efficient way to run the Community's legislative programme. Six months of the presidency is too short to prepare the legislative programme and shepherd it through. Too much is really expected of national civil servants who only once every six years have to take initiatives and manage the conduct of the Council. The lack of continuity is a major handicap in the efficient conduct of Community affairs.

The question is whether one could not arrive at a longer or even more permanent leadership of the Council and, at the same time, link relations between Community institutions more closely. One possible suggestion would be to appoint or elect the President of the Council to hold office for the duration of the life of the Commission and Parliament. A senior European statesman commanding general respect amongst governments might be acceptable as the permanent chairman who would furthermore head the permanent secretariat of the Council. He could stand as one of the two vice-presidents of the Union on the ticket of an elected President of the Commission, suggested above.

Under this system the presidents of the Community's three principal institutions would be a team, committed to the same overall programme for which they would have obtained a general mandate directly from the citizens of the Community. Of course the detailed programmes of legislation and the conduct of Community affairs would continue to be accountable to and require the approval of the Council and Parliament.

The Parliament

This leads us to the consideration of the balance of powers between the Council and Parliament. The European Parliament succeeded a nominated Assembly of national parliamentarians which, under the various treaties, was largely confined to an advisory role. It became directly elected in 1979 and consists of 518 full-time members whose powers have, however, increased only very slowly.

It has the right to dismiss the Commission by a vote of censure, but cannot censure individual commissioners. On budgetary matters it shares powers with the Council and agreement between the institutions is necessary for the budget to be adopted. The legislative role of the Parliament remains essentially advisory, though the Council cannot enact legislation without first consulting the Parliament. Theoretically this could have allowed the Parliament to block legislation it did not like. However, under the Single Act these powers have now been extended. Over most issues covered by the Act the Parliament can now amend or reject legislation proposed by the Council. In such an event the Council has to act by unanimity if it wishes to override the Parliament's objections. As a result, on a number of specified issues, the two institutions have now moved closer towards a process of co-decision over legislation.

A significant gap still exists over the democratic accountability of the Community to its citizens, compared with that enjoyed in relation to their elected national, regional, and local governments. Although the European Parliament is directly elected, its powers certainly do not match those of national parliaments. The Council, which is still the principal legislative organ of the Community, cannot be collectively held accountable for its actions.

As long as Council decisions required unanimous agreement, each minister could, theoretically, be held answerable for his decisions in his national parliament. Once majority voting applies, especially behind closed doors, no individual minister can be personally held accountable. And the collective decisions of the Council cannot be subjected to scrutiny by the individual twelve national parliaments – to whom the Council is not constitutionally responsible.

If the Community's actions and decisions are to retain democratic legitimacy, then the directly elected European Parliament must acquire legislative powers equal to those of the Council. Co-decision, now exercised over a few specified issues, should be extended to the whole field of Community action. Detailed recommendations about how this should apply are included in the Parliament's Draft Treaty.

Other institutions

One of the important remaining institutions of the Community is the Court of Justice, based in Luxembourg, whose thirteen judges and six advocates-general ensure that Community law is applied and obeyed. Then there is the Court of Auditors which oversees the accounts of all Community institutions and bodies set up by them. Finally there is an Economic and Social Committee, a purely advisory body which must, however, be consulted by the Commission and Council over a wide range of issues. It consists of three interest groups, generally described as the social partners. The first group represents employers, the second workers, and the third various interests including consumers, farmers, the self-employed, academics, etc. Its members, nominated by governments, are appointed for renewable four-year terms.

Whilst there seem to be no grounds for changing the composition, powers and functions of these three remaining institutions, there is one further gap that ought to be filled. If the federal principle of interdependence between the different levels of government is considered desirable, then a formal relationship ought to be established between the Community institutions and the sub-national levels of government in the member countries.

Informal contacts with regional and local authorities already exist. The regional affairs Commissioner, for instance, consults a representative body of these authorities on issues of concern to them in his area of responsibility. Yet Community decisions affect the interests of local communities and their citizens in most other spheres. It seems logical that they should be subject to the same principle of consultation as that laid down for the groups represented in the Economic and Social Committee. Occasionally local government representatives have been included amongst its members, but that is really not good enough.

There seems to be a clear case for establishing another formal Community institution, representing sub-national tiers of government, with consultative powers similar to those enjoyed by the Economic and Social Committee. There is already in existence a prestigious and representative body called the Council of European Municipalities and Regions, which enjoys formal consultative status within the Council of Europe. It represents several thousand municipalities drawn from all the twenty-two countries of the Council of Europe. This organization could provide suitable nominees for such a new Community institution.

Not all the institutional reforms suggested above would be necessary to transform the present Community into an effective democratic Union or Federation. The key is, however, the extension of legislative co-decision to the European Parliament in all matters not yet covered by the Single European Act. Without it the Community lacks democratic legitimacy and remains largely subject to the whims and personal prerogatives of heads of national governments and ministers subordinate to them.

Chapter eight

Towards one Europe

The sudden and dramatic collapse of the communist regimes in central and eastern Europe lifted the iron curtain that divided the European continent for over forty years and brought to an end the armed confrontation between two incompatible economic and political systems. As a result the security and political relationships between east and west are undergoing a fundamental change. The year 1988 saw the signing of the first disarmament treaty removing a whole class of intermediate nuclear weapons from Europe. Since then large unilateral cuts in troops and equipment have been taking place within both the Atlantic and Warsaw Pact alliances. Further disarmament negotiations to limit strategic nuclear arms and achieve parallel reductions in force levels are making good progress.

The reforms within the Soviet bloc started when Mikhail Gorbachev came to power in 1985, and have been gathering momentum ever since. They signal the end of totalitarian rule and the progressive transformation of most one-party communist states into pluralist democratic countries, operating social market economies. This has, in effect, brought to an end the ideological confrontation between east and west that has dominated our lives ever since the Second World War.

The west's positive, if cautious, response to these dramatic developments could lead to an entirely new system of common security in Europe. The ultimate objective is to remove armed confrontation and the threat of conflict from the European continent for good. How do we go about it? The lessons of the past five decades might offer a way forward.

The Second World War ended with Europe's economy totally dislocated and on the point of collapse. The dominant powers in Europe were the United States of America and the Soviet Union. The latter, as devastated economically as the rest of the continent, maintained its dominance by military occupation. In their alliance, aimed at defeating Nazi Germany, capitalist America and Britain on the one hand and Marxist Russia on the other subordinated their differences, but the alliance did not long survive the end of the war.

Churchill, in his Fulton speech in 1946, spoke of the consequences of Europe's division into two politically incompatible camps and urged a policy of strength and unity in the west. The division became explicit with the Soviet rejection of the Marshall Plan and the forceful imposition of communist governments in all the countries which they occupied.

Fearing further Soviet expansion, Britain, France, and the three Benelux countries signed a joint defence pact in March 1948 in Brussels. Following the Soviet blockade of Berlin, negotiations took place to establish a North Atlantic security system. In April 1949 the USA and Canada signed the North Atlantic Treaty with ten European countries, including the five Brussels Treaty signatories and Denmark, Iceland, Italy, Norway, and Portugal. Greece and Turkey joined in 1952, Germany in 1955 and Spain in 1982.

From then on, the world's two competing super-powers directly confronted each other in Europe, armed to the teeth and ready for instant war. To maintain their security both sides tried to sustain sufficient armed forces to deter each other. The mutual deterrence no doubt helped to provide some forty years of peace in Europe, though at considerable risk and cost. Purely military protection has always been unstable, for security gained through greater armed strength by one side makes the other insecure. Thus the arms race is sustained and ever more sophisticated strategies are developed to justify it. Each upward twist of the arms race increases the risk of accident or miscalculation.

Genuine security means much more than military balance. It requires the development of mutual trust between countries, treaties whose observance can be monitored and machinery for the peaceful settlement of differences. Beyond that it should extend to co-operation in economic, social and political spheres, leading to a growing interdependence between nations which ensures permanent common security.

The goal of common security was, after all, the main motivating force behind the decision of the European countries, after the war, to unite to put centuries of internecine war behind them. The European Community, by developing common interests, policies, laws, and institutions, has become the embodiment of such a system of common security. War between its member states is now inconceivable: it is no longer feasible.

Is it then possible to create a similar system of common security for the whole of our continent? Such a proposition would have invited derision during most of the past four decades. But it is no longer unthinkable. The escalating cost of modern weaponry has put immense pressure on both super-powers to reduce their defence expenditure and commitments. The American contribution to the defence of Europe, through NATO, costs some $150 billion a year, equalling the massive current US budget deficit. Political pressures in America will inevitably lead to reductions in their defence expenditure on Europe. The Soviet Union's huge defence commitment, said to devour some 12 per cent of GNP, has starved the domestic market of scarce resources. With *perestroika* and *glasnost* – in other words, fundamental reform in full public view designed to break out of economic stagnation and backwardness – the Soviet government has already taken major international initiatives to reduce the need for their heavy defence expenditure.

Disarmament

These pressures have led the two super-powers to negotiate the INF Treaty, covering the removal of a whole class of intermediate nuclear weapons from Europe. Further major reductions of strategic nuclear weapons are being sought through the START negotiations. The Soviet government has also proposed to negotiate the removal of short-range and tactical nuclear weapons in Europe, reduce conventional arms and ban chemical weapons. It withdrew its troops from Afghanistan and is offering to promote regional peace settlements in other parts of the world.

The new strategy adopted under Gorbachev's leadership appears to focus on ways to avert world war, to advance towards a conventional military balance and to forgo any plans that may have existed to invade western Europe. This has led to agreements on scrapping nuclear weapons under dependable on-site inspections and control. In 1986 Gorbachev proposed substantial reductions in ground and air forces. In 1987 the Political Consultative Committee of the Warsaw Pact recognized the need for asymmetrical reductions in conventional forces and arms to equal levels on both sides. Furthermore it recommended the adoption of a new defensive military doctrine. This would include reducing conventional forces in Europe 'to the level where neither side, in ensuring its defence, would have the means for a surprise attack on the other side or for mounting general offensive operations'. As a token of his intentions Gorbachev announced at the United Nations in December 1988 the unilateral reduction of Soviet forces in Europe by some half a million troops and the destruction of several hundred tanks.

The Soviet proposal to remove its capacity to wage an offensive war, the threat of which has dominated east–west relations in Europe for forty years, is momentous. The potential of the proposal has been compared to President Sadat's journey to Jerusalem in 1977 and the subsequent peace settlement between Egypt and Israel.

The first reactions in western Europe to these remarkable developments were anxiety and disbelief in the honesty of Soviet intentions, coupled with a resentment against the Americans for negotiating over

European heads. There was fear that disarmament in Europe would reduce and possibly even remove American commitment to its defence, exposing Europeans to Soviet pressure. Individual countries such as Britain, France, and Germany each responded in different ways to the INF Treaty, threatening disunity within the Atlantic Alliance. The British wanted to modernize nuclear arsenals to replace the potential that had been negotiated away. The French feared that the resulting *détente* could lead to a separate Soviet deal with the Germans. Alarm at further arms reductions exposed differences with the Germans, who were anxious, now that the intermediate weapons had gone, to remove short-range battlefield nuclear weapons that would obviously all explode on their territory in the event of war. There was a general fear of the unknown after forty years of comfortable security under the American umbrella.

Changes in the East

Western European fears and hesitations waned with the progressive collapse of communist governments in central and eastern Europe in 1989 and 1990. The first non-communist government emerged in Poland when candidates nominated by the *Solidarność* movement won, in the June 1989 general elections, 99 per cent of the seats in the upper house and practically all the freely contested seats in the lower house. Reserving for themselves and their coalition allies 65 per cent of the seats in the lower house, the communists hoped to retain power. But they were abandoned by their coalition partners who, by switching support to *Solidarność*, enabled the latter to form a new government. At the start of 1990 it introduced revolutionary economic and monetary changes aimed at a rapid transformation of the command system into a market economy. It brought spectacular results. Inflation running at some 80 per cent in January dropped to single figures within three months. The Polish currency became fully convertible, and goods not seen for decades became readily available, though at much higher prices. On paper living standards fell by a third or more, but in reality the drop was less dramatic. Previously there was plenty of money but nothing to buy for it. The return to a market-based economy meant that there were now goods available to match the purchasing power of the population. Unemployment, however, is growing and so are new inequalities between haves and have-nots, creating social strains, strikes, and unrest among the less-favoured sectors like the farmers. Nevertheless support for the government continues at very high levels and there is no risk that the process of economic reform will be reversed. If anything, pressure is growing to move forward to a full market economy even faster. Poland's biggest problem remains with the vast foreign debts incurred by the previous regime. Interest and capital repayments, unless substantially alleviated and postponed, could stifle the economy and threaten the survival of the present government. The emerging pluralist democracy might well be undermined and, in the search for other solutions, a new authoritarian nationalist regime, of the type that ruled Poland between the world wars, could re-emerge.

Hungarian reforms designed to move towards a market-based economy started much earlier than in Poland, but failure by the communist government to relinquish control over the main sectors of the economy or allow large enterprises to meet the full force of competition, stifled earlier improvements. Economic decline resulted in pressure for political change and led to the toppling of Janos Kadar, the communist leader of the country, installed by the Russians after the abortive 1956 revolution. After intensive internal debate and a number of governmental changes, the general elections held in May 1990 resulted in a defeat of the communists and the emergence of a non-communist coalition government, determined to cut all links with the previous regime. It negotiated the withdrawal of Soviet troops and aims to leave the Warsaw Pact and its economic organization Comecon. Whilst the Polish shock remedies have been rejected, economic reforms towards a full market system are moving apace.

The revolution in Czechoslovakia was bloodless. The student-led protests in Prague brought about the rapid collapse of the government and its voluntary acceptance of non-communists into leading government positions. The communist-dominated parliament elected the dissident playwright Vaclav Havel as president only a few months after his release from jail. The June 1990 elections resulted in a massive victory for the non-communist parties. A new coalition government headed by an ex-communist is introducing economic reforms at a steady pace. A relatively low level of foreign indebtedness and the experience of a rather successful industrial economy before the Second World War promise a manageable conversion into a full market economy. Withdrawal of Soviet troops has been negotiated and the government is championing a new system of common security in Europe to replace the Warsaw Pact.

In contrast, the Romanian revolution at the end of 1989 was far from peaceful. The execution of the dictator Ceausescu and his wife by the army, which refused to suppress the anti-government demonstrations that erupted throughout the country, did not, however, lead to the rejection of the communists. Those who gained power had all been members of the previous regime and have continued the old methods of suppressing democratic protest. The May 1990 general elections did not follow Polish, Hungarian, or Czechoslovak examples. The non-communist parties, harassed by government-backed forces, failed to overturn the communist majority which under a new name, the National Salvation Front, won 66 per cent of the seats, while its leader, Ion Illiescu, was elected president with 85 per cent of the vote. Although practically free from foreign debt, the economy is at a very low ebb, poverty is widespread, and living standards wretched. Social protest and ethnic unrest between Romanians and the large Hungarian minority in Transylvania continue to erupt and threaten both internal stability and relations with neighbouring Hungary.

Change in Bulgaria has not been as dramatic as in the rest of eastern Europe. The communist dictator Todor Zhivkov was deposed by his party in November 1989 after thirty-five years of rule. The party changed its name and the new leaders, although they had held senior positions in the old regime, declared themselves its opponents, in favour of multi-party democracy and a market economy. In the June 1990 elections they won nearly half of the votes well ahead of their nearest non-communist rivals. Whereas in other eastern European countries communists were regarded as collaborators of a hated foreign power, Bulgarians have always looked to their Russian Slav brothers for support against the Turks, and there are no Soviet troops in Bulgaria. Thus communism and nationalism were not incompatible and the deeply traditional rural population distrusted the less experienced city-based intellectuals standing for the opposition. Gradual economic change is the order of the day.

The collapse of authoritarian communist regimes all around them have had far-reaching effects on the cohesiveness and stability of the Yugoslav federation. Not tied to the Soviet bloc since the late 1940s, successive Yugoslav communist governments, starting with Tito in the 1960s, introduced reforms aimed at decentralizing the command economy and moving towards a socialist market system that has not really worked. After Tito's death the highly centralized political system at federal level began to loosen and the constituent republics have been seeking ever greater autonomy. Internal economic failure and the collapse of communist systems elsewhere finally precipitated separatist tendencies. Slovenia, with the highest living standards, threatened to leave the federation and apply for European Community membership. Croatia, after electing a non-communist government in 1990, wants to follow Slovenia's example The largest republic, Serbia, tries to assert its dominance over the semi-autonomous province of Kosovo with its almost entirely Albanian population. The Serbs, forming the largest ethnic group within the federation, have ambitions to extend their influence over the whole country. Internal ethnic conflicts and divisions are threatening the very survival of the federation in its present form, whilst extreme nationalism and ethnic unrest continue to grow.

Instability within Yugoslavia is in some ways a mirror image of the growing instability within the Soviet Union itself. From a tightly and centrally controlled command economy, Soviet political and economic reforms aimed at devolving power have suddenly lifted the lid off previously suppressed separatist national and ethnic ambitions of the Union's wide mix of races, nationalities, languages, cultures, and religions. The fifteen republics are all seeking greater autonomy and some want outright independence. The failure, hitherto, of the economic reforms and the continuing fall in living standards are increasing the strains. Political and social unrest including armed conflicts in the southern republics are seriously threatening the cohesiveness of the Soviet Union itself. The prospect seems to be the emergence of several practically independent republics linked, at best, within a much weakened federation.

German unification

The collapse of the communist regime in eastern Germany carries, however, the most far-reaching consequences for the future of Europe. The dismantling of the Berlin Wall was a signal for the end of a divided Germany. Once the communists were defeated in the March 1990 elections there was no further reason to maintain the existence of a separate German state in the east. Unification, as rapidly as possible, became the goal of all political forces in both Germanys. Monetary Union in July 1990 was quickly followed by a full political merger in October. The democratic transformation of the eastern German economy, financed by the west Germans, will be painful for the hundreds of thousands losing their jobs. But it will be rapid and could provide a pattern and example to other central and eastern European countries trying to become market economies themselves.

Initial reactions of Germany's western allies to the prospects of unification were anxious and hesitant. Countries within the Warsaw Pact, with the consequences of the Second World War in mind, were fearful and hostile at first. The prospect was of a united Germany of some eighty million inhabitants, economically the most successful and prosperous country in Europe, becoming the preponderant power on the continent. Genuine fears were expressed by some, in the west as well as in the east, that what Germany had failed to achieve by force of arms under Hitler, she would now be able to secure by economic domination. A united, sovereign, independent, and powerful Germany in the centre of Europe seemed to pose a renewed threat which its divided status over the previous forty years had effectively removed.

History has, however, moved on. The Federal Republic is a founder member of the European Community. It has always been one of the strongest protagonists of the Community's transformation into a

European federation, and this objective is actually spelt out in the German constitution. The French, mindful of their history of past wars and conflicts with the Germans, were the first to react. They recognized that, even within the existing Community, a united Germany could become the dominant partner, dictating its future course and development. That is why France's President Mitterrand called for the speeding up of progress towards a full economic and political union within which national sovereignties would be pooled and no single country could impose its will. The Germans responded enthusiastically and support for Mitterrand's call followed from most other Community countries. As a consequence the European Council of heads of governments agreed, in April 1990, to convene an intergovernmental conference on Political Union at the end of the year, to be held in parallel with the one aimed at Economic and Monetary Union. Thus German unification provided the principal and a powerful spur for faster progress to full European Union. This is now likely to result in a new Treaty to be signed before the end of 1992, coming into effect during the 1990s.

Common security

German unification raised another major issue. As a member of the Warsaw Pact, the German Democratic Republic, hosting some 380,000 Soviet troops, formed the bulwark of the Soviet defensive *cordon sanitaire* against any military threat from the Atlantic Alliance. The absorption of the GDR by the Federal Republic and its prospective switch to NATO was seen as a direct threat to the Warsaw Pact. Indeed the Polish government, unlike the Czechoslovaks or the Hungarians, declared itself in favour of retaining Soviet troops on their territory for the time being and not letting the Warsaw Pact dissolve.

With the ending of the ideological divide between east and west, the Soviet Union and its allies, anxious for closer economic and political co-operation with the west, have been the prime movers for the development of a new system of security in Europe which could replace both the Warsaw Pact and NATO. The framework for it is seen to be the Conference on Security and Co-operation in Europe (CSCE) to which practically all European countries now belong, including the Soviet Union as well as the USA and Canada. Their objective was achieved by a treaty signed by all CSCE members in Paris in November 1990 reducing armed forces in Europe to levels of non-provocative defence, guaranteeing all existing frontiers against the threat of armed aggression and securing the means of enforcement of the treaty provisions. This new security system could, in the view of the Warsaw Pact members, lead to the replacement of both existing military alliances.

NATO members are more hesitant. The dramatic changes within the Soviet bloc have shattered its previous stability imposed by coercive power. Future developments in the east, whilst hopeful, are raising new uncertainties and dangers to peace and stability in Europe. That is why the west must not over-react in its approach to the changing circumstances. To maintain stability, change has to be managed wisely and gradually, while safeguarding against any fundamental reversal of current trends within the Soviet Union. As reliance on instant military action is reduced by cutting forces and arms, there must be parallel developments of effective mutual on-site inspection and confidence-building measures. Confidence building needs to extend from purely military measures to economic and political co-operation. As the west's interests lie clearly in a continuation of the Soviet Union's political and economic reforms, the west could well help the Soviet leadership sustain them. Closer political and economic ties with the Soviet Union are essential if the Soviet Union is to stop relying for its security on the military occupation of eastern Europe.

Europe as a whole has an overriding interest in encouraging these developments. The separation of central and eastern Europe since the Second World War has in no way lessened their peoples' kinship with European culture or their desire to come closer to their western neighbours. The development of the European Community, although officially largely ignored by communist governments, has excited much interest amongst the more informed of their citizens. Given the opportunity, most of them would join the Community with little hesitation. The European Community should equally have no hesitation in welcoming into membership other European countries able to accept its rules and obligations. Indeed the prospect of ending the artificial divisions imposed after the war and uniting the whole of our continent has always been a long-term hope and objective of the architects of European Union.

The European Community must therefore develop a clear vision and policy to take advantage of the opportunities being offered by disarmament and apparent political changes in the east. The first task is to recognize the need for a common strategy. The Community's strength and security depends on its unity. Instead of its members being at the mercy of events which, separately, they can do little to control, they can together shape their future by negotiating as one with both the United States and the Soviet Union. This is the only way to ensure that Europe's fate will not be decided 'over our heads' and that the Soviet Union will not gain in political advantage what it surrenders in military terms.

The Atlantic Alliance

Progressive disarmament is bound to change the nature of the present Atlantic Alliance. If the Americans are not to be driven into pre-war isolation there must be a gradual strengthening of a western European security identity, while a dialogue develops with the east. Continued, even if modified, American participation in the defence of Europe is more likely to be encouraged by the existence of a militarily unified Europe within the Atlantic Alliance.

What then are the policies which western Europe needs in order to build a stronger pillar within the Atlantic Alliance and promote common security? The task, expressed by Lord Carrington, the Secretary-General of NATO in March 1988, is 'the search for a system of security which meets the needs of east and west at much lower levels of arms and armed forces than at present'.

Europe's greatest fear has centred on Soviet superiority in conventional arms. The Soviet offer to negotiate asymmetrical reductions should be pursued positively, since any further reduction of nuclear arms, now aimed at deterring conventional attacks, will depend on whether a balance of conventional forces can be achieved. Then nuclear weapons would only be needed to deter the threat of a nuclear attack. The Russians have offered to negotiate the reduction of all conventional arms and forces between the Urals and the Atlantic under full inspection, search, and supervision. The fear of forces being brought from Asia over the Urals could be allayed by an American commitment to send troops across the Atlantic in response.

Movement towards a conventional balance would make it much easier to negotiate the removal of short-range tactical nuclear weapons from central Europe, a step much wanted by the Germans. Western nuclear deterrence at intermediate level would remain based on existing aircraft-borne bombs, and the missiles carried in submarines.

The control and reduction of strategic nuclear and space weapons is now under negotiation. Uncontrolled development of a new weapons system like the American Strategic Defense Initiative (so called Star Wars) is clearly against European interests. European countries are unlikely to join the race to develop the next generation of nuclear defence systems, which would threaten Europe's existing space satellites and nuclear weapons and introduce new instability in relations between the super-powers.

If the Americans and Russians secure an agreement for the first 50 per cent cuts in their respective strategic weapons, under the START talks, this might well lead to discussions for further major cuts. That would then be bound to bring French and British nuclear forces into the negotiations. Inclusion in such negotiations does not necessarily mean giving them up altogether, but negotiating upper levels for the number of French and British warheads would secure a minimum nuclear deterrent at a level that Europe would probably wish to retain as long as the two super-powers also remain nuclear powers. The numbers of warheads and their ratios as between the Americans, Europeans, and Russians are a matter for negotiation.

If a comprehensive nuclear test ban were negotiated, indicating an end to the nuclear arms race, then the climate might well be created for substantial cuts in weapons on all sides. Under present French and British plans for modernization, the number of warheads under their control would rise from the present 125 each to some 500 each. The USA and the Soviet Union now possess some 10,000 warheads each, or forty times the European level. If the two super-powers were to cut theirs, below their suggested 50 per cent reductions to, say, some 2,500 each, raising the European level to 1,000 would not seem justified. In such circumstances a combined minimum European deterrent of, say, some 200 warheads, based on submarines, would secure a credible but non-threatening nuclear defence for western Europe as long as NATO and its American strategic nuclear umbrella remain in being.

Reductions of this order, coupled with a general nuclear test ban, would enhance the case for a stronger non-proliferation treaty, which is under review. Whilst the existing Treaty has limited the emergence of new nuclear powers to China, many other countries possess the capacity to develop their own nuclear weapons. The existing nuclear powers have therefore the highest incentive to prevent further nuclear proliferation and place the world community in a position where no individual country could, with impunity, threaten others with their use.

If sufficient confidence were established between the two super-powers plus Britain, France, and possibly China, a new concept of common security in the nuclear field might emerge. An agreement to place their nuclear capabilities under a supranational World Security Authority with the strictly limited powers of deterring any country from the use or threat to use nuclear weapons anywhere throughout our planet, might ultimately lay to rest the fear of nuclear war ever breaking out. Such a development is more credible than existing proposals merely to ban nuclear weapons. As long as countries retain their sovereignties in the field of defence, no effective guarantee would exist against cheating. Only the ultimate emergence of a world community with its own government, capable of enforcing its decisions, would make the total removal of all nuclear weapons in our world possible and acceptable to those countries that already possess them.

The European pillar of NATO

In spite of progress towards a common security system in Europe likely to emerge from the CSCE negotiating process, there is genuine reluctance within NATO to see its own demise. Its members do not want to see the USA decouple itself from Europe, but recognize that the relative decline of American economic power must lead to the progressive reduction in its military preponderance within the alliance. To counteract this the European Community, or at any rate its members that belong to NATO, need to build a more cohesive European defence identity.

This means the creation of an effective European defence pillar with a number of developments. One prerequisite is common arms procurement. Progress towards this is described in chapter 4. If requirements are to be rationalized and economies in research and development achieved, there must be a single European defence budget for research and development and the joint arms requirements will have to be determined by a European arms procurement agency. This could be created out of the present Independent European Planning Group (IEPG) but with a Director General and a permanent Secretariat.

The second requirement is a much closer military integration of the forces of the European allies. NATO forces are already remarkably well-integrated, but what is still missing is the full integration of the French and Spanish forces within a common infrastructure, command system, and with common strategies. The French armed forces of 300,000 and its nuclear deterrent plus some 200,000 Spanish troops, fully integrated into a common defence force, would greatly strengthen the European pillar of the Alliance.

Even though French opinion has in recent years moved towards closer participation in the western alliance, it is unlikely that France would be prepared to return to the NATO command structure. This explains developments which include the setting up of a Franco-German Defence Council and a common brigade. Helmut Schmidt in his Adolphe Bentinck Lecture in Paris in February 1987 proposed the replacement of NATO forces in Europe by a Franco-German army under a French general and a French nuclear umbrella. British, Italian, and Benelux forces could become associated. The Atlantic link would be maintained through the presence of two or three American divisions on the European continent. This proposal, however, is only piecemeal and begs many questions.

The key lies in developing a common philosophy on defence and its role within possible political developments in east–west relations. There is need for a common assessment of the perceived threat of aggression and the balance of forces needed as well as a clear political objective for constructive change in relations with eastern Europe and the Soviet

Union. For this, western Europe needs effective political machinery to put its strategies into practice and to negotiate as one with both the Americans and the Russians.

To do all this there is need for a common institutional framework within which France and Spain can be fully integrated into the defence of Europe and in which western European defence, and foreign and economic policies, are managed as a coherent whole. The revival of the Western European Union, based on the 1948 Brussels joint defence pact, may well provide the answer. This already includes nine Community members (Benelux, Britain, France, Germany, Italy, Portugal, and Spain) and might possibly be extended to other NATO countries belonging to the European Community. Its role as a centre for reflection on security problems, and concerted action, makes it an appropriate forum for security matters within the Community's European Political Co-operation. Indeed the Single European Act has laid down that EPC should co-ordinate political and economic aspects of security. At the same time NATO's European activities within the Eurogroup and the Independent European Programme Group (IEPG) could be brought under the WEU umbrella which could provide them with a permanent secretariat. This would interlock NATO and the European Community through WEU. The ultimate aim would be the fusion of WEU and the European Community within a European Union that has its own common defence and foreign policies.

Moving towards this objective requires a transitional phase with a timetable for its implementation. The General Staffs of member countries would be asked to formulate a common European security concept, with various options, to provide a European role within NATO and for further integration of Europe's defence forces. A European defence research and development budget would have to be set up to enable the proposed European Arms Procurement Agency to determine and implement a programme for the development of weapons for common defence. The Secretariat of European Political Co-operation, established under the Single European Act, should acquire the right of initiative like that of the European Commission, in anticipation of its ultimate merger with the Commission.

The political role of negotiating with the Americans within the Atlantic Alliance would thus move to the European Community's own institutions. The same would apply to the negotiations between the Community and the Soviet Union and their allies. The way in which Community institutions should acquire the capacity to conduct a common foreign policy is discussed in the next chapter. We confine ourselves here to discussing policies aimed at achieving a system of common security in Europe.

The first issue concerns relations with the USA. There is a fear that

117

closer European integration within NATO risks American decoupling. The fear has been partly fed by American disapproval of the revival of the Western European Union and suspicions about its aims. If, however, the policies emerging from WEU and EPC clearly show that Europe is ready to take greater responsibility for its defence, then the Americans would be reassured. After all, criticism of Europe's alleged failure to shoulder a fair share of the burden of defending itself has been growing in America. The more integrated its defence forces, the more effective they will be.

The Atlantic Alliance would be strengthened even if, as a result of their greater cohesion and independence, European policies and perceptions of their common interests were to differ from those of their American allies more often than they do at present. A united Europe could also take on some security responsibilities outside the NATO area, as often urged by their American allies. Indeed, the involvement of the whole of NATO in providing the military means for the enforcement of UN sanctions against Iraq provides the first example of the involvement of the Atlantic Alliance outside Europe. Unity in Europe might therefore bring about a new common relationship with America that extends beyond Europe to other parts of the world. Negotiations between the Americans and the Europeans on a more equal basis are more likely to safeguard the alliance with a common aim of achieving a system of global security.

Enlargement of the Community

The second problem concerns the Community itself and its possible enlargement to include countries that are not part of the Atlantic Alliance. At present Ireland alone does not belong to it, and espouses a policy of neutrality. The Irish have, however, accepted the Single Act which provides for the co-ordination of political and economic aspects of security. To permit their abstention from decisions on security issues, the Act contains a clause which enjoins members to refrain from impeding the formation of a consensus and the joint action this could produce. Pronouncements by Irish politicians have recognized that the emerging European Union will increasingly gain a security dimension as part of the common foreign policy it is developing, and that the Irish will not dissociate themselves from it.

If the division of the European continent into the two military alliances confronting each other is replaced by an over-arching common security system that includes both alliances, as well as European countries that belong to neither, then new opportunities for European integration arise. Members of the European Free Trade Area (EFTA) have been increasingly concerned about their exclusion from the Single

European Market and its decision-making organs. Negotiations for the creation of a European Economic Area between the EC and EFTA have the object of securing the full access of the latter to the single market. Whilst the Community concedes to them the rights of consultation, it is unwilling to admit EFTA countries into the governing organs of the Community itself or allow them to block the system of majority voting. The system is based on a careful formula, which now applies to the enactment of most legislation concerned with the implementation and operation of the single market; in consequence EFTA countries, while enjoying access to the single market, could not have the right to participate in decisions about its operation.

EFTA member countries are, of course, entitled to apply for full membership of the Community, but most of them have not done so because they have hitherto felt that membership would compromise their neutral status. Of EFTA members only Norway and Iceland are members of NATO. Norway, having rejected membership in a referendum in 1972, is now anxious to join, but is reluctant to break ranks with its Norwegian partners. Austria, Finland, Sweden, and Switzerland are explicitly committed to neutrality. In spite of its neutrality Austria has already broken ranks and in 1989 applied for membership. Should a common European security system emerge in which the EFTA countries could participate then the principal objections of the neutrals to full European Community membership would largely disappear. There are thus good prospects that most EFTA countries will apply to join within the next few years.

Other potential candidates for membership are Turkey, Cyprus, and Malta, all of whom have already submitted applications. Pending further political reforms establishing full human rights and genuine democracy in Turkey, and the resolution of the Turkish occupation of northern Cyprus, the Turkish and Cypriot applications are likely to remain on ice. The Maltese application is still to be considered. In any case the European Community has made it clear that no new members are likely to be admitted until the completion of the single market after the end of 1992.

Then there are the countries of central and eastern Europe that have abandoned the communist system and are trying rapidly to convert themselves into full market economies. Although they have successfully detached themselves from dictation by Moscow and re-established their political independence, they are most anxious to develop the closest economic relations with their western neighbours and the European Community in particular. They are fully aware that, without substantial help from and co-operation with the west, their economic transformation will be difficult to achieve – with internal, social tensions and conflicts threatening the very survival of their new pluralist democratic political systems.

Recognizing the dangers but also the opportunities in the east, the west, including the USA, entrusted the European Community with channelling help to the new democracies in the east. The European Bank for Reconstruction and Development (EBRD) with an initial membership of some forty countries was established for this purpose. It is, however, becoming increasingly clear that much more needs to be done if the transformation of central and eastern European countries into pluralist democratic market economies is not to fail. The post-war American Marshall Plan was one example of how shattered economies in Europe were helped to help themselves rebuild their prosperity. The current experience of the transformation of the east German economy within a united Germany could be even more relevant. The nature and scale of the reforms needed are similar and the German example could act as a guide in mapping out the type of help needed by the rest of central and eastern Europe. Quite apart from the economic benefits likely ultimately to flow back to the donors of an imaginative and generous programme of help, which would create vast new markets for their exports, a rapid and successful transition of the economies of the recipients would safeguard democracy. Failure risks the resurgence of extreme nationalism, social and ethnic unrest, the re-establishment of authoritarian regimes, and threats to stability and peace in Europe.

Looking beyond the economic transformation of their countries, most of the governments involved have declared their interest in participating in the process of European co-operation and integration. They have applied to join the Council of Europe, and a number of them, including the Soviet Union, have already been accorded observer status in anticipation of full membership once they have adopted fully democratic pluralist political systems.

The majority of the central and eastern European countries have, furthermore, declared their intention to seek full membership of the European Community once their economies have been reformed and reached a level enabling them to accept its rules and obligations.

The political pull of integration within the emerging European Union has, paradoxically, an even greater attraction for them. Although they have succeeded in re-establishing their independence and sovereignty by breaking away from the Moscow-dominated Soviet empire, they are aware that in our rapidly shrinking world total political and economic independence is no longer relevant or possible. Furthermore, like the EFTA countries, they can also see that only full participation within the European Community would ensure an effective say and share in decisions, to which they will increasingly become subject even if they remain outside the Community. The emerging European federation in which decisions are shared for some matters but national autonomy is reserved for most other issues, and in which distinct cultural identities are fully guaranteed and maintained, offers an attractive alternative to the uncertainties of unfettered national sovereignty that would exclude them from an increasingly interdependent world.

The response of the European Community to their interest has been to propose a form of association which would not guarantee ultimate membership, but provide a framework for economic co-operation that could, as in the case of EFTA, lead to full free trade with the Community. Whilst the Community is understandably hesitant to open its doors to a large number of new members there are grave political dangers in excessive caution. Firm expectations of full economic and political membership of the Community would provide these countries with a definite political objective. They need this clear perspective if they are to combat disruptive nationalist tendencies and risks to the survival of their still fragile democracies. The offer of full membership within a reasonable time scale would act as a powerful factor of political stability and a safeguard against any attempts at authoritarian alternatives that would prejudice their prospective membership of the Community.

It took seven years from the date of their application for Spain and Portugal to join the Community. With this lengthy transition as an example, is it not possible and indeed advisable for the Community to be much more positive? It should offer an assurance to those central and eastern European countries that wish to join that, subject to the necessary economic transformation and the maintenance of political pluralism, they would be admitted to membership of the Community within a specified number of years but not later than by the end of this century. Nothing would contribute more to the confidence of those countries, speed up internal reforms and safeguard their democracies, than a clear goal within a defined term of years of full membership of the emerging European Union.

Relations with the Soviet Union

Full European Community membership for the Soviet federation, even if it were a fully democratic market economy, is not really within the realm of practical politics. The Soviet Union is still a nuclear super-power with a population close to that of the Community itself, with a land mass stretching from eastern Europe right to the Pacific Ocean. Its membership would totally change the nature of the Community and put into question the careful political and constitutional balance between its present medium-sized and small member countries. The likely further enlargement of the Community after 1992 to EFTA countries and further east, that might have to accommodate ultimately perhaps double its current membership, will require further institutional reforms,

121

checks, and balances. This is amongst the subjects of the negotiations for Political Union that started in December 1990.

The future relationship with the Soviet Union requires a different direction. The Community's interests lie with helping the Gorbachev administration to achieve its internal reforms, if these are likely to lead to a decentralized market economy and political freedoms. The reforms are not only likely to benefit the Soviet people, but should secure reduction of international tensions, stimulate trade, and foster closer co-operation.

A positive policy of help and co-operation from the west that brings tangible economic benefits to the Soviet people will furthermore strengthen the hands of the present reformers and help their successors to prevent the system from slipping back into its bad old ways. Such a policy would need more than the benevolent cheering from the sidelines that characterizes most current western reactions to Gorbachev's efforts.

The Soviet Union needs to increase its trade with the west, particularly in technologically advanced goods, to help speed up the modernization of Soviet industry. The Russians have called for western enterprises to set up plants under joint-venture agreements. There is a case for many more exchanges, including the training of management and technical personnel. Contacts like these, coupled with much greater cultural links, will increase knowledge and understanding and inevitably encourage a more open and pluralist society in the Soviet Union.

More needs to be done, however, if growing co-operation between east and west is not to be arrested, or even reversed by the toppling of the present leadership and a return to a more closed and repressive regime. If future co-operation and the developing system of common security is to be assured, the Community's own origins might provide some signposts.

The principal motives of the founders of the Community were to make future wars between its member countries impossible. They achieved this objective by progressively integrating their economies, starting with the placing of the coal and steel industries under supranational control. The choice of coal and steel was designed to remove from national control basic industries which were then essential for military re-armament.

At the present crucial stage in Europe's history a similar imaginative leap forward could well provide safeguards for the mutual security for which both sides of our Continent so clearly yearn. Today it is coal, oil, gas, and nuclear power that generate modern economies and fuel the armed forces. Already our common needs for energy transcend our divisions. In spite of past American opposition, Siberian gas now flows through pipelines into western Europe and Polish coal generates some of our electricity. The use of fossil fuels has at the same time been responsible for much of the pollution that is threatening our environment. Nuclear energy poses other major threats, highlighted by the Chernobyl disaster and the almost insoluble problems of nuclear waste disposal.

Suppose that these primary sources of energy were to be brought under international control with the aim of effecting their rational development and safe use for the whole of Europe, east and west; and that the conservation of our common environment, so much dependent on the methods of generating energy for industry and transport, were to be similarly controlled. An independent Energy and Environment Authority established on the basis of equality between the European Community, the Soviet Union and any other interested European states, whose decisions were binding on all participants, would introduce a novel supranational element into European relations. Its existence and the acceptance of its rulings would generate trust and could lead to a rapid extension of economic co-operation with the Soviet federation.

The European Community's own early experience showed how the habit of working together, and growing interdependence, made it impossible for President de Gaulle to reverse the process when the French withdrew from the Community's Council of Ministers for several months in 1965. The benefits of membership proved too strong and persuaded him back to the negotiating table and, after the so-called Luxembourg compromise, to the continued development of the Community.

Were an east–west European Energy and Environment Authority to be established, is it not also likely that growing co-operation and interdependence would soon make the process irreversible? Mutual benefits would surely outweigh any arguments in favour of the re-erection of barriers and a renewal of confrontation, whoever happened to be in charge in national capitals. The trust generated could ultimately, as in western Europe today, make military confrontation between individual countries or groups of them not only unnecessary but quite irrelevant.

Even if differing political and economic systems were to continue to divide us, such differences might in the long run be no greater or more threatening than existing linguistic or religious differences within our own countries. These may sometimes lead to quarrels or conflicts as in Belgium or in Northern Ireland but, however regrettable, they do not threaten our very survival. East–west interdependence might not remove all ideological rivalries, but could well make obsolete all armed conflict between us in Europe and lead to a permanent system of common security. It would furthermore make it more likely that the Soviet Union would not fear or object to those of its eastern European

123

neighbours who wished to do so joining the European Community. It would, furthermore, bring the Soviet federation into as close an economic and political relationship with the European Community as that enjoyed by the USA, and create a new partnership between all three federations that could provide an example for an ultimate global settlement.

Chapter nine

The Community and the world

We live in a world that has shrunk in all except its purely physical dimensions. Not only are we instantly aware of major political, economic, social, or physical events taking place anywhere in the world, but we are directly or indirectly affected by most of them. The very survival of humanity is at risk should a nuclear conflict ever break out. Parts of our planet could become uninhabitable for thousands of years in the event of major nuclear accidents, of which the Chernobyl disaster was such a terrible warning. Political and economic rivalries have precipitated two world wars this century. The cold war era of confrontation between the capitalist and communist camps could well have led to a third one. Smaller and more local conflicts between countries provide a constant threat of spreading and drawing in others.

Economically we have become increasingly interdependent. Self-sufficiency is either a necessity confined to very poor and isolated communities, or a means of escape for groups of individuals nostalgically anxious to recreate economic and social conditions of allegedly happier and more primitive past societies that did not rely on the 'benefits' of technology and modern civilization. For the rest of us, life is largely dependent upon outside sources for food, energy, and raw materials.

Even Europe as a whole cannot subsist on its own resources. The European Community depends for most of its energy on imports of coal, gas, and oil from countries in other parts of the world. It is the biggest food importer and most of the raw materials for its industries come from over seas. Uncontrolled exploitation and depletion of finite resources could eventually deprive our industries of the means to continue supplying our daily needs.

Large parts of our globe and indeed the whole of humanity could be damaged by ecological changes brought about by our own actions. Massive air, water, and soil pollution, destroying our forests, poisoning our lakes and crops, and crumbling our buildings, is with us already. Deforestation is the main cause of major flood disasters and the spread of barren deserts that in recent years have resulted in large-scale famines. Global warming, caused by carbon dioxide produced by the burning of coal, oil, and gas, is a distinct possibility. Over the next two or three decades global temperatures could increase by 4.5°C. This would raise ocean levels by some 1.4 metres and flood vast expanses of land. Ozone layer depletion due, amongst other causes, to the use of chlorofluorocarbons in aerosols and refrigerants could lead to the escalation of cancer related diseases and the disruption of the ocean food chains.

The international arms trade, highly profitable for suppliers, is generating and sustaining conflicts in all parts of the world, with ever more sophisticated weapons increasing the scale of death and destruction. Illegal trade in arms is feeding terrorism, that has emerged as the violent alternative to peaceful reform within and between countries. International trade in narcotics and drugs, in spite of stringent border controls, appears to be growing all the time. And no border controls, however sophisticated, can stem the epidemic of AIDS that is now threatening millions of lives throughout the world.

Serious problems on the world's agenda are multiplying and need effective action at global level. Yet the world's existing institutions are often much too weak and divided to face up to the issues. Some 150 independent and sovereign states belonging to the United Nations find it difficult to co-ordinate their actions or reconcile their differences so as to resolve problems common to them. What is missing is the willingness and capacity to subordinate individual interests to the common good. International institutions need to be endowed with supranational powers and sanctions so that their decisions become enforceable international law.

It is in this area that Europe offers a unique example. The European Community has been founded on the principle that its laws not only take precedence over national laws but, when enacted, themselves become national laws enforceable by the judiciary in each member country. It is the agreement of members to cede elements of their national sovereignty to the Community that has enabled it to enact common legislation and ensure its observance. Whilst it may be a long time before the world community will be ready to emulate Europe's example, the European Community could do much to help advance it.

Foreign policy

The Community's interest in proselytizing its own methods and structure is fairly obvious. Interdependence generated by integration has made war between its members not only unthinkable but no longer practicable. Europe's living standards, as the world's largest trader, largely depend on the preservation of peace in the rest of the world. Thus any measures which reduce the risks of war must be of primary concern. Conservation of the world's natural resources is equally important for the world's biggest importer of food and raw materials. Growth in its own prosperity depends on the living standards and purchasing power of its trading partners rising too. That is why the European Community, more than most, has a direct interest in helping developing countries to grow out of their poverty. That is also why the European Community should have a single foreign policy actively pursuing its common interests.

How, then, can Europe play a world role that is commensurate with its potential? In wealth, expressed in its total gross domestic product, the Community is now second to none. Coupled with its share of world trade it is an economic giant, but politically it is still a pygmy. The reason is that, except for issues of trade and external commercial relations, foreign policy does not yet form part of the Community's own responsibilities. All that has happened up to now is that in certain limited fields foreign policies of individual member states are being co-ordinated. The original Rome Treaties made no mention of foreign policy. A degree of co-operation in foreign affairs was achieved only as a result of the Davignon Report of 1970 which recommended a system to 'harmonise points of view, concert attitudes and, where possible, lead to common decisions'.

Acceptance of the Davignon Report led to the development of so-called 'political co-operation'. For several years this involved quarterly meetings of foreign ministers, kept strictly separate from Community business, though more recently both types of business have tended to be transacted at the same meetings. In addition, Political Directors, appointed by each foreign minister, met every month with day to day communications assured by a special telex system.

The Single European Act has finally codified the system by formally committing member states to 'endeavour jointly to formulate and implement a European foreign policy'. This is to be achieved by close consultation on any foreign policy matters of general interest, so that convergence of positions and joint action could follow. The European Commission and the European Parliament are to be fully associated with the proceedings of political co-operation. Finally every effort is to be made to ensure that the external policies of the European Community concerned with economic affairs should be consistent with foreign affairs pursued under the system of European Political Co-operation. To help the administration a secretariat, under the direction of a committee of the Political Directors of member countries, has been set up in Brussels to prepare and implement the activities of European Political Co-operation.

In practice, political co-operation has developed in three main areas. First there is a commitment by the twelve member countries to try to speak with one voice at international meetings. Thus in the United Nations the foreign minister of the country exercising its six month presidency, speaks on behalf of all member states during the annual opening debates of the General Assembly. The twelve ambassadors to the UN take a lot of trouble to co-ordinate their policies and vote together. Common positions are also presented at other international gatherings, of which the various conferences arising from the 1975 Helsinki Agreement on Security and Co-operation in Europe have been prime examples.

Second, on several occasions common action was agreed on the imposition of economic sanctions. These included sanctions against Southern Rhodesia in 1965, against Iran in 1980 after that country took American diplomats and their staffs as hostages, against Poland after the imposition of martial law in 1981, against Argentina during the Falklands war in 1982, against Israel after the invasion of Lebanon in 1982, and against South Africa in 1986. In August 1990 the Community committed itself to back the United Nations resolutions on the Middle East crisis following Iraq's invasion of Kuwait.

Finally a stream of declarations has been issued by the Heads of member governments on a whole host of issues, including the Middle East, the Gulf War, Afghanistan, Central America, South Africa, and east–west relations, but to little effect. In a few cases the declarations have been followed by diplomatic missions by foreign ministers of countries holding the presidency of the Community, with no more effect.

Clearly until the Community as such can speak and act as one in foreign affairs its capacity to influence world events will remain minimal. So much effort is expended on trying to co-ordinate foreign policies of member states that what emerges tends to represent consensus at the lowest common denominator of agreement. A typical example has been that of sanctions against South Africa. Minimal measures with little effect on that country were agreed in the face of British objections to the imposition of any sanctions whatsoever. Another weakness of trying to negotiate common attitudes is that, as a result, Europe usually only reacts to events instead of taking foreign policy initiatives.

The contrast between Europe's passive and ineffective role in foreign affairs and its well developed and active external commercial policy is striking. This can be explained by the differences in the way policy is formulated and decisions are reached for the two areas of external affairs. Commercial policy is formulated by the European Commission and its proposals require a qualified majority in the Council to become Community policy. It is highly unlikely that the Community will be able to speak and act effectively before the system of decision-making in foreign affairs conforms to that of its external commercial policy. Responsibility for the formulation of external policies should therefore be transferred to the European Commission. Its proposals would ultimately have to become subject to qualified majority voting in the Council, even if for a transitional period unanimous agreement of member governments would still be required for some aspects of policy.

In dealing with this issue the European Parliament's Draft Treaty for European Union draws a distinction between 'common action' and 'co-operation'. The former is in fields where the Union has exclusive or concurrent competence with member states. This applies to commercial and development aid policy and to those external policies which fall within the exclusive competence of the existing Community. It covers the Union's relations with non-member states and international organizations in which the Union would be represented by the Commission. Decisions on common action are taken by a qualified majority vote. Co-operation covering other aspects of foreign policy and the political and economic aspects of security would, under the Draft Treaty, be subject to unanimous agreement and its conduct would remain under the direction of the Council. Formulation of policies and proposals for action would, however, also become the responsibility of the European Commission. The European Council, representing the heads of governments, would have the right to extend the field of co-operation to issues not previously handled by the Union, such as defence policy and trade in arms. It could furthermore decide, on the proposal of the Commission and with the Parliament's agreement, to transfer areas of policy from co-operation to common action. A commitment to endow the European Community with powers and institutions to conduct its own foreign policy is the subject of the inter-governmental conference on Political Union convened in December 1990.

North–south

Even before more competences for external affairs are transferred to the European Community's own institutions, much more can be done in the economic field where the Community is already largely responsible. Apart from issues of peace or war, dealt with in the previous chapter, it is the north–south divide that presents the greatest threats and challenges to humanity today. The Community has a better record in this field than most other developed countries, but much more needs to be done to tackle underdevelopment in the Third World with its damaging consequences for all of us.

Despite progress over the past twenty years, some 3,000 million people live on an annual income that is less than the monthly income of people in industrialized societies. In many countries it is no more than one fiftieth of that enjoyed on average in the European Community. The consequences for the poorest are malnutrition, illiteracy, unemployment, illness and epidemics. Some 400 million children already suffer from serious nutritional deficiency.

The principal causes of underdevelopment stem from high birth rates and the underemployment of the expanding population, as well as from limited or underexploited natural resources. Most Third World countries are not able to satisfy their own basic needs, let alone export surpluses to enable them to buy the products they lack. Owing to population growth, the Third World's cereal imports grew from 25 million to 80 million tonnes between 1960 and 1980 and could grow to more than 200 million by the end of this century. Inadequate local food prices discourage production, whilst climatic disasters such as floods or droughts can destroy several years' work. Through indiscriminate exploitation of such resources as forests and inappropriate cultivation of cleared lands, the natural environment is being gradually destroyed in many parts of the world. Each year an area twice the size of Belgium turns to desert. At this rate one quarter of the earth's surface is in danger of becoming a desert within twenty-five years. The vast watershed of the Himalayas is being transformed as forests are felled to provide more agricultural land. The deforested area no longer absorbs the snows and monsoons, which lead to massive floods that have devastated Bangladesh. Tropical rain forests are being felled and burned indiscriminately at a rate which, if continued, will result in the total disappearance of rain forests within eighty-five years. Some of them in West Africa, Malaysia, Indonesia, and the Philippines are unlikely to survive much beyond the end of this century.

Many Third World economies, operating under a system first established by and for their former colonial masters, have depended for their exports on just a few primary products needed by the richer world. Between the 1950s and the 1980s prices of many primary products fell by more than half in real terms. Such worsening of the terms of trade have led to a massive imbalance between imports and exports, a reduction of purchasing power, and a growing deterioration of the financial position of poorer countries. To survive, they have gone into deep debt with high interest rates. The total debt of developing countries by 1988 was some $1,300 billions, equivalent to not far off double their annual export earnings. On average interest payments absorb nearly one fifth of these.

For some heavily indebted countries interest payments absorb up to half of their export earnings.

To break out of this vicious downward spiral urgent action must be taken by the rest of the world community, and especially the rich countries of Europe, North America, Japan, and Australasia. The priorities are: combatting hunger and protecting the environment from further destruction, dealing with debt, stimulating trade, production, and investment, and generally assisting regional development.

The European Community's own record to date has not been bad, but limited in geographic scope. The origins of its policies towards Third World countries stemmed from the agreement in the original Rome Treaty to associate former Belgian, Dutch, French, and Italian colonies with the Community. With British, Spanish, and Portuguese accession the number of former colonies so associated increased and now some sixty-six countries in Africa, the Caribbean, and Pacific (known as the ACP countries) are linked under the so-called Lomé conventions, which are renegotiated every five years. These are administered by common institutions on a basis of equality between the Community and its Third World partners.

Under the conventions some 99.5 per cent of the goods exported to the Community by the ACP countries are free of customs duties, with no reciprocal concessions required on their part. Some exceptions relate to farm produce, which enjoys protection under the CAP, and quantitative limitations on textiles under the Multifibre Arrangement. Development aid includes both grants and low interest loans and has risen to some Ecu $8\frac{1}{2}$ billion for the latest five-year period up to 1990. A particular feature of aid has been the so-called Stabex fund which compensates countries heavily dependent on one or more staple products for severe fluctuations in their export earnings. A similar system, called Sysmin, applies to mineral products.

The aid is concentrated on rural and agricultural development, on projects assisting small and medium-sized enterprises, and on feasibility studies for industrial projects and productive infrastructure such as ports, railways, water supplies, and telecommunications. The Lomé conventions are not, however, to be regarded as charitable. The Community's self-interest, so dependent on the supply of basic commodities and raw materials from the Third World, lies in the rapid development of poorer countries that will in due course provide valuable markets for Community products.

Whilst priority is given to the ACP countries, aid and trading concessions are also granted to other Third World countries. The aid falls under two categories. The first provides food and emergency aid to countries suffering from natural catastrophes or other crises. Then there are bilateral agreements, under which development aid is included, with such countries as India, Pakistan, Bangladesh, and Sri Lanka, and, in Latin America, with the five members of the Andean Pact and the six countries of the Central American isthmus.

Trade concessions are principally under a system of generalized preferences which are granted to all developing countries without discrimination and are not reciprocal. They involve the total suspension of customs duties, subject however to quota limits or ceilings which are reviewed each year to take account of the growth of international trade. They apply to all finished or semi-finished industrial products and to some 400 processed agricultural products.

Co-operation agreements which give duty-free access to most industrial products and specific concessions for agricultural produce have been negotiated with some twelve Mediterranean countries (i.e. all except Albania and Libya), and with the six countries of the Association of South East Asian Nations (ASEAN).

All the Community's programmes of assistance to the Third World represent an impressive effort, accounting for some 40 per cent of all world aid given, but they still fall far short of the UN target of devoting at least 0.7 per cent of GNP to aid. Of all the member countries only Denmark and The Netherlands have reached the target. Furthermore, the Community's agricultural policy has encouraged the dumping of food surpluses on world markets, at times in competition with Third World farmers. Much more needs to be done if the agreed objectives of the Community's policies towards the Third World are to be realized.

The highest priority must clearly be given to action to eliminate the causes of hunger. China and India have been most successful in ending their recurrent famines. The problem is largely confined to Africa. What we need to do is to help to individual farmers to improve their skills, encourage appropriate land reform, set up proper marketing systems, build roads, and increase prices to producers so that they will stay on the land. Under the Lomé Convention the Community should do a deal with the appropriate ACP countries so that increased development aid will be directed towards agriculture in return for a co-ordinated programme designed to achieve the outlined objectives.

Both in the context of combating the causes of hunger and in helping development generally, high priority must be given to safeguarding the environment. In return for debt relief measures, developing countries would have to guarantee to maintain their stock of renewable resources and conserve those that could not be renewed. Funds would only be released for projects which conform with laid down environmental criteria. A multinational World Environment Trust should be set up which, again in return for debt relief, would acquire and preserve rainforests and generally control the exploitation of environmentally sensitive commodities.

At the initiative of British and French governments some progress was made in dealing with debt relief at the September 1988 IMF/World

Bank meeting for thirty-four low-income African countries. These involve writing off one-third of the official debt and extending the repayment period, cutting the interest rate by half, or extending the debt for a further twenty-five years with a fourteen year grace period. Other measures ought to supplement these arrangements. A modified system of debt relief could be offered if its 'servicing' is done in local currency. The proceeds could then be channelled into a Development Fund to finance agricultural, social, and environmental investment needing local currency. A European Development Corporation, funded from new Community resources and the European Investment Bank, should be authorized to purchase discounted private banking debts of developing countries in return for which the latter would undertake to carry out conservation measures suggested above.

In addition to aid, debt relief and investment, the principal contribution that the Community can make to help developing countries out of bankruptcy and to build up their economies is through increased trade. This involves a further opening up of the Community's own markets, helping to promote trade between developing countries amongst themselves, and by playing a positive role within the United Nations Conference on Trade and Development (UNCTAD) to improve the functioning of the international system. To increase purchasing power and employment within Third World countries, European industry should be encouraged to enter into production-sharing arrangements with local enterprises, and a European Community Export Credit Agency should be established, with uniform credit rates for imports from the Community. In all these trading transactions the Ecu should be used, as it would provide a more stable currency for trade with the Community and amongst developing countries themselves.

Finally, the Community should take the initiative of developing its relations with potential regional leaders and the regions they represent, such as Brazil, Mexico, India, China, Egypt, Nigeria, and the ASEAN countries. The objective should be to encourage the co-management of the world's most urgent problems and to assist them to grow into viable economic regions. More united, the regions would be better able to tackle common problems of environmental breakdown, indebtedness, and trade through the development of payments unions, trade financing agencies, and common institutions to handle relations within regions. The Community itself should help in major regional environmental actions such as, for example, the plan for the Brahmaputra basin. In all these actions the European Community can play a crucial role in leading the world out of poverty and its present divisions, towards a greater unity of purpose.

Relations between rich countries

In its relationship with the richer northern world the European Community has an equally important role to play to bring stability and economic growth. During the first three decades after the Second World War, the world's economy developed in a way unequalled before or since. It grew within an international framework consciously established to promote growth. The GATT was designed to free trade, and the Bretton Woods System and the IMF to secure exchange rate stability and adequate resources to overcome balance of payments problems. The European Community itself showed the massive benefits of economic integration. Trade between its members grew twelvefold in twenty-five years, while world trade grew fivefold.

The devaluation of the US dollar in 1972, the development of floating exchange rates, and the quadrupling of oil prices and those of most raw materials following the 1973 Israel/Arab war, slowed growth and introduced new barriers to trade through wild currency fluctuations, fuelled by speculation and vast, volatile flows of capital. Trade and investment suffered, whilst high rates of inflation forced deflationary policies. With the breakdown of monetary stability, protectionism reared its ugly head again, while excessively high exchange rates eliminated competitive industries in some countries. One result has been mass unemployment at levels not seen since the 1930s. Another was growing parsimony in aid towards the Third World. US aid, for instance, tumbled from 2.4 per cent of its GNP in 1948 to 0.2 per cent during the Reagan administration, and much of what remained is in the form of military assistance, whereas US contributions to world agencies have been cut drastically.

What can Europe do to reverse the trend and bring back some greater order to international economic relations? Already, by having a single identity in trade and commercial relations with the world outside, the European Community has succeeded in changing the balance of power and contributing towards the establishment of a more orderly world system. The Dillon, Kennedy, and Tokyo rounds of tariff reductions, and the success with which the worst features of protectionism have been kept at bay during the past decade, have been due largely to the Community's single voice in trade matters and the influence it brought to bear as an equal partner of the Americans. In contrast the lack of a common European role in monetary or macro-economic policies, quite apart from foreign and defence policies, has meant that its influence has been much less effective on the international scene.

A Monetary Union achieved through the development of the European Monetary System, strengthened by British participation, with the Ecu becoming Europe's currency under the control of a Central

Bank, would give Europe an equal voice with Japan and the USA. In their common interests, the three major world currencies would find it easier to move towards exchange rate stability. By promoting greater harmony between their respective macro-economic policies they would be able to reduce the uncontrolled movement of capital in the international financial markets. Closer co-operation could lead to the strengthening of the IMF and the World Bank, including the development of new assets to fuel and sustain the growth of world trade. Finally, an economically united Europe would have more self-confidence to promote freer world trade and combat protectionist tendencies amongst their main trading partners.

Political Union

The case for the European Community to act as one in defence of its interests throughout the world is obvious. That is why the extension of its competences to all aspects of foreign policy, including defence, is urgent. A European Political Union with a common foreign and defence policy would transform the world scene fundamentally. Some might fear the emergence of another super-power, but as the world's largest trading unit, which is also strategically vulnerable, Europe must be capable of defending and furthering its interests. These include a further reduction of trading barriers. The European Union should also want to see the developing countries grow economically and thus offer new markets for Europe's exporters. Monetary and economic stability would provide the framework within which a new world economic order could emerge.

European initiatives to encourage regional unity in Latin America, Africa, and Asia, on lines similar to those pursued within Europe, could help other continents to reduce local conflicts and promote regional co-operation. Growing economic interdependence within regions and between them would lay the foundations for a world free from local or general wars. Common global problems such as the protection of the environment and conservation of the world's scarce resources would be easier to pursue. It would also be easier to curtail indiscriminate trade in arms, promote international action to combat the drugs trade, and organize effective measures to defeat terrorism. The habit of co-operation would demonstrate that a world order guaranteeing peace and growing prosperity is within reach. From there the next step could be to provide the whole of our planet with a system of enforceable international law under the authority of a world government with strictly limited, but real powers.

Chapter ten

Europe's future

History is shaped not so much by events as by circumstances leading up to them and by reactions to them afterwards. This definition helps to explain the reasons for European integration and its progress and can assist in charting the probable course of events to come. The reaction to the carnage of the First World War was an attempt to regulate international relations by voluntary agreement between fully sovereign nation states within the League of Nations. The ideas floated then about creating a European federation to prevent war and promote co-operation were not accepted or even understood. The League failed in its objectives because it lacked authority and sanctions to enforce its decisions. The lessons of its failure, which led to the Second World War, were, however, learnt, and former enemies in Europe decided to create supranational institutions whose decisions would become legally binding upon the participating states.

The European Coal and Steel Community, set up in 1951, implemented the principle of supranationality by establishing a High Authority that was independent of governments. Whilst its institutional system was of a pre-federal nature, Robert Schuman, in his declaration which led to the establishment of the ECSC, saw it 'as a first step in the federation of Europe' but he also recognized that 'Europe will not be made at once or according to a single overall plan'. Against the background of the cold war in Europe and actual military conflict in Korea the next obvious step in European integration seemed to be in the field of defence and political unification. It led to the signing of the European Defence Community Treaty in 1952 and negotiations for the establishment of a European Political Community in parallel. However, the lessening of international tension, following the death of Stalin in 1953, removed the urgency for defence integration and, following the failure of the French Parliament to ratify the EDC Treaty, progress towards political and defence unity was arrested.

The impetus towards unity was maintained, however, by building on the success of European economic co-operation, stimulated by the

Marshall Plan which led to the establishment of the Organization for European Economic Co-operation and the European Payments Union. Successful negotiations that followed the collapse of the EDC Treaty resulted in the treaties setting up the European Economic Community and EURATOM. This time the treaties were ratified and came into force in 1958. The timetable for the setting up of the common market under the EEC Treaty was not only kept, but actually implemented ahead of its target date.

In the meantime, however, the collapse of the Fourth French Republic, which brought General de Gaulle to power in 1958, had a profound though temporary effect on the development of the European Community. France was its leading member and de Gaulle was opposed to supranationality. As long as he remained in power further progress towards European unity was delayed. Once he resigned in 1969 the process was restarted. The Community was enlarged from six to nine members. It acquired its own financial resources and resolved to achieve a European Union by 1980.

Progress towards it was marked by commitment to move towards Economic and Monetary Union and to the development of political co-operation. But the world oil crisis in 1973 and the massive rise in prices of most primary products stimulated a rapid rise in inflation and major monetary instability. Efforts to construct the Economic and Monetary Union collapsed and progress to full Union was delayed. Agreement was, however, reached to elect the European Parliament by direct universal suffrage and to make another attempt at monetary unification through the establishment of the European Monetary System in 1979.

The process towards political unification followed. Yet another solemn declaration to transform all relations between member states into a European Union was signed in Stuttgart in 1983 by ten Heads of Governments (Greece having joined in the meantime). The European Parliament produced its own Draft Treaty for European Union in 1984. This resulted in the Single European Act which came into force in 1987, after its ratification by the national parliaments, now numbering twelve as Spain and Portugal had also joined the Community. Finally, it has led to the firm commitment to negotiate the establishment of a full Economic, Monetary and Political Union of Europe.

The story so far illustrates that progress towards some form of European federation, commenced in 1950, has proceeded ever since, even if by stops and starts. The stage of integration already reached, over a relatively short period when measured against other major developments in world history, has been quite remarkable. Each major step forward in the process hitherto has, after all, depended on unanimous agreement between participating states, none of whom was forced to agree.

Consequences of the Single Act

The stage reached with the coming into force of the Single European Act brings about a qualitative change in the process of integration. This is due largely to the firm commitment to drop the practice of unanimous agreement before enacting legislation. This has already resulted in the adoption of so many decisions that, in the opinion of the February 1988 Summit conference, progress towards a single integrated European market is now irreversible. Its achievement by the end of 1992 or soon afterwards is thus pretty well assured. The future course of integration will be determined by the direct consequences of a unified European market and the nature of the reactions to it.

The creation of a single market without internal frontiers and with full freedom of movement for capital, goods, services, and people will transform the Community economically into the equivalent of a single country. Such a market can no more be left to its own devices than those of individual states. These manage their markets by legislation and its implementation by governments and their agencies. Regulation of the market requires competition policies that prevent abuses and promote efficiency in its operation, provide choice and freedom to trade. Laws are enacted covering the structure and conduct of enterprises engaged in industry and trade. The need for such regulation at Community level is already recognized but, clearly, as frontiers between member countries are removed, all other barriers to the achievement of a single integrated market must also go. The regulations have to cover all existing differences between countries that could impede the operation of a unified market, including protectionist measures such as public procurement and subsidies that discriminate in favour of national interests. The necessary legislation becomes the responsibility of the European Community's legislative organs and its implementation that of its executive Commission acting directly or through individual member governments.

One of the most important barriers to a fully integrated market is the continued existence of individual currencies that fluctuate against each other. Fixing them as in the European Monetary System is a step in the right direction. But they will not stay fixed unless national economic policies are fully co-ordinated. The role of guidance for such co-ordination will increasingly fall yet again to the European Commission. In effect, for the management of the market and co-ordination of economic policy the European Commission will have to assume the role of a government for economic affairs.

Another essential step is the development of the Ecu as a genuine currency for all normal purposes of trade and exchange within the Community and with the outside world, possibly first alongside existing national currencies and ultimately replacing them altogether. Such a currency must, however, be managed in the same way as individual currencies of member states. This has to be done by a central or federal bank that will control its issue. Whether such a bank is independent, as in Germany, or subject to some governmental control, as in most other Community countries, is a matter for further debate. It will be an institution operating on behalf of the whole Community and not subject to national control.

Other barriers which will have to go are major differences in taxation that affect free trade between member countries. Their approximation is already recognized by all member states as indispensable. Even the British government, that opposes their approximation by agreement between member states, hopes that the objective would be achieved by market pressures alone.

Every individual member government pursues policies aimed at assuring economic and social cohesion as between different parts of its country and sectors of activity. Most countries try to even out inequalities and disadvantages – caused by uncontrolled market forces between its regions – by controls, subsidies, and national investment in transport and infrastructure, and through the redistributive effect of national taxation on regional incomes. Much of national legislation in the social sphere is also designed to promote cohesion and even out gross inequalities between different sectors and people; so is legislation for minimum standards of health, consumer protection, and for the alleviation of poverty and destitution. Once the European market is fully integrated, similar measures promoting economic and social cohesion will have to be applied for the Community as a whole.

In competition with other parts of the world the Community will be able to keep up its end only if national industrial and technological barriers are replaced by policies promoting a unified Technological Community with common standards, shared research and development, and common procurement by public authorities, especially in the field of defence equipment. The Community's external policies, now only exercised in the field of commerce, will have to be extended to the whole gamut of economic relations, once the Community becomes responsible for guiding its economy and for its currency. In effect the Community would then be conducting its own foreign economic policy which could not, ultimately, be separated from the spheres of politics and defence.

Public opinion

Are people ready to accept these objectives and the changes needed to achieve them? Very substantial and comprehensive data is available on public attitudes to Europe. Ever since 1973 the European Commission's

Directorate of Information has been commissioning independent research institutes to conduct extensive public opinion surveys twice a year. All the institutes employed belong to the European Society for Opinion and Market Research, which lays down strict standards for their members. The surveys conducted in Britain are by Gallup Poll. The sample for each survey is about 12,000 interviewees carefully divided by population numbers between 138 regions within the Community of twelve countries. To secure results that would ensure less than a 5 per cent margin of error, not less than 1,000 interviews are conducted in each member country, with the exception of Luxembourg where the figure is 300. Fifteen years of polling have confirmed their accuracy by the relative closeness of responses to identical questions in consecutive surveys, illustrating both the consistency and trend of opinions.

The so-called Eurobarometers of opinion provide extensive data on a wide range of issues of interest and have shown that generally opinions throughout the Community are fairly similar between its different member countries. Larger variations which show up often relate to the length of a country's membership of the Community. The six original members often appear more enthusiastic about Europe than some of the latecomers such as Denmark and the United Kingdom, though not Ireland, Spain or Portugal whose opinions are closer to those of the Six.

Each survey includes questions on the future development of the Community and the data quoted below are confined to those issues. A major survey on the future of Europe was published in March 1987 on the thirtieth anniversary of the signature of the Treaty of Rome and the following responses were recorded on questions of direct relevance to our analysis of public attitudes:

Question: Are you personally for or against the European Community developing towards becoming a United States of Europe?

Of those who replied, 76 per cent were in favour throughout the Community. The figure for the original Six EC members was 83 per cent. The United Kingdom figure was 58 per cent. Denmark alone had a majority of 60 per cent against.

Question: After what time would you entrust the government of Europe with the responsibility for the economy, foreign affairs, and defence?

The responses to those who chose the timescale of 'in the next twenty years' were 65 per cent throughout the Community. In the UK the figure was 58 per cent of those who replied.

Question: In the case of an election for the head of government of Europe, is it possible that you would vote for a candidate who was not of your nationality or would you rule it out?

Excluding those who expressed a conditional opinion, 69 per cent throughout the Community said yes as against 31 per cent who would rule it out. The comparative figures for the UK which were the lowest amongst the twelve show 54 per cent saying yes with 46 per cent opposed.

On the more complex question of national against a European identity the survey sought attitudes on a graduated scale between the following two opinions on which interviewees were asked to indicate to which opinion they found themselves nearer:

Some say (A): If one day the countries of Europe were really united, this would mark the end of our national historic, cultural identity, and our own national economic interests would be sacrificed.

Others say (B): The only way of protecting our national historic, cultural identities, and our national economic interests against a challenge put up by the Great World Powers is for the countries of Europe to become truly united.

Of those who indicated an orientation towards one or the other of the above statements, excluding those who chose a middle position, the results showed 72 per cent throughout the Community favouring proposition (B) and 28 per cent favouring (A). The corresponding figures for the UK were 54 per cent for (B) and 46 per cent for (A). The only country showing a clearly adverse attitude to European unity was Denmark.

What these responses show, as do answers to many more questions that appear regularly in the twice yearly Eurobarometers, is that a substantial majority of Community citizens are ready to see progress towards European Union. The least enthusiastic are the Danes, but even they, when faced with substantial progress towards this goal in the Single European Act, accepted it in a referendum to which the issue was submitted in 1986. As for British public opinion, this certainly appears to be in advance of many of their political leaders.

Definition of the United States of Europe

The question then arises about what is actually involved in creating a federal United States of Europe? Since its start in 1950 progress towards this objective is clearly well beyond the half-way stage. The Community has supranational institutions including an embryo government in the form of the executive Commission, a fully empowered legislature in the Council of Ministers, a body of laws that are applicable throughout the Community, and a Court of Justice whose rulings on constitutional issues and on individual laws are final and binding.

The directly elected Parliament, while having to be consulted on all

Community issues, has as yet only limited legislative powers. Existing Community responsibilities extend to a wide range of economic and social issues including full responsibility for the conduct of external commercial relations. The foregoing chapters in this book set out the present extent of the Community's powers and responsibilities.

What then are the changes and reforms necessary to transform the present Community into a full federation? As the Community's history shows, it will not happen overnight nor by a single major reform. The process is continuous and usually emerges as a reaction to, and consequence of, previous changes and advances. The significance of the present stage of the Community's evolution lies in the Single European Act and the consequences of its implementation. The transformation of the economic Community of twelve member countries into a single economic unit, which heads of governments have recognized by now as irreversible, requires major and consequential changes in the way in which a unified economic area has to be governed. The suggested changes appear under the various chapter headings and the most important ones are summarized below.

The most immediate need, as capital movements are liberalized and the Ecu becomes an increasingly widely used European currency, is the establishment of a Federal or Central European Bank to control the issue of the Ecu and to play a co-ordinating role in the Community's monetary affairs. As the European market becomes fully integrated into a single economic area, the existence of several national currencies operating and being managed independently cannot be sustained. Not only have all the currencies to be fixed against each other, as in the existing European Monetary System, but their occasional re-alignments should be reduced to the minimum by co-ordinating the economic policies of members states at the European level. Once currencies have ceased to fluctuate and the Ecu is being used widely for both official and private transactions, the stage will have been reached for the Ecu to become the sole European currency.

The effective completion of the internal market will depend not merely on the removal of all barriers to trade including, in particular, the enforcement of common public procurement, but also on a co-ordinated and adequately financed European research and development programme for all advanced technology. To match the industrial and technological potential of its principal technologically advanced competitors in the non-military field, the Community should try to pattern its co-ordinating role on that of the Japanese Ministry of International Trade and Industry. In the field of defence, it should develop common arms procurement as well as a space programme which, as in America, would stimulate technological innovation that would bring benefits throughout industry.

Financing the suggested European research and development programme and common arms procurement needs financial resources that are not available to the Community under its existing budgetary arrangements. Whilst effective reform of the agricultural policy may well reduce its predominant claim on the Community budget, there will be a growing call for the saved financial resources to be used to even out regional and social divergences that, in a fully unified market, are likely to widen. In particular, effective investment is needed for improved transport links with, and the development of the infrastructure of, the least favoured regions of the Community. Basically what is needed is adequate European finance to promote greater cohesion. This is not a plea for more public spending. On the contrary, twelve separate national expenditure budgets on research and development, arms procurement, and regional and social aids, are bound to be much more costly and wasteful than financing single and co-ordinated policies in these areas. That is why an enlarged Community budget replacing much of the duplicated national expenditures could actually bring about major savings in public finance. Furthermore a progressive system of Community taxation, related to the wealth of member states and their citizens, once spent on its programmes for regional and social cohesion, would have a significant redistributive effect and reduce the gap between the richer and poorer regions and sectors.

A budget of between 5 and 7 per cent of the Community's gross domestic product, according to the MacDougall Report referred to in chapter 5, could have such a significant redistributive effect. Much more effective democratic control than at present of public expenditure at Community level would have to accompany any increase in its revenues. If the European Parliament and the Council of Ministers were actually responsible for raising taxes for the Community, which would directly impinge upon the taxpayers instead of coming out of national budgets, they would act more responsibly in controlling expenditure.

The Community budget would become even more significant if research and development and common procurement in the defence field became its responsibility. This raises the whole issue of integrating Europe's defence efforts and developing a common security policy. The arguments for such a development are deployed in chapter 8. In the rapidly changing international scene, following current disarmament negotiations and the American pressure for Europe to bear more of the financial burden of the Atlantic Alliance, a common European defence policy becomes ever more urgent. Only when Europe speaks with a single voice in its relationship with the USA can it become an effective partner of the USA and an equal pillar of the alliance.

The profound changes that have taken place as a result of the collapse of the communist system within the Soviet bloc open up entirely new

143

perspectives for the European Community. A common European security system could end the division of our continent and replace confrontation by increasing co-operation between east and west. Neutral countries, members of the European Free Trade Area would lose their principal objections to full Community membership. The newly emerging central and eastern European democracies, helped to transform themselves into market economies, would also become eligible for Community membership. Finally there are the political and economic developments taking place in the Soviet Union. The Gorbachev reforms signal major possible changes in east–west relations, particularly in Europe itself. If western Europe is to play any significant role in influencing developments and responding to the challenges and opportunities which the economic and political changes in the Soviet bloc and system offer, then the Community must have a common foreign policy. This should have clearly defined objectives aimed at the ultimate removal of Europe's division into two halves confronting each other, that has dominated our lives since the Second World War. A constructive relationship with the Soviet Union of growing economic co-operation leading to interdependence should be a clear objective.

With a common foreign policy, Europe will be able to make a much more significant contribution to world affairs. Its interests as the world's largest trader depend on global peace and genuine economic growth, particularly in the developing world. Europe's interest in the latter is already shown by its 40 per cent share of all aid advanced to the Third World. The faster it grows the bigger its markets for Community products and services. That is why Europe has a direct interest in finding solutions to the debt burden that inhibits further growth and development. Some solutions might well combine help to the debtors in return for their action to safeguard natural resources such as forests, the depletion of which is threatening our global climate and environment.

Europe has an even more significant role to play in changing international relationships and laying the foundations for a new world order with common governance. The experience of the European Community's own origins and progress towards a federation offers an example to other regions in the world that, like Europe, have suffered from conflicts and divisions. The Community has a unique vocation, based on its own experience, to promote regional unity in other parts of the world. Co-operation between integrating regional groups of countries could lead to the emergence of a world authority – with the capacity and power to promote balanced economic growth, conservation of the global environment, and world peace – that would banish for ever the threat of a nuclear holocaust or, indeed, of any armed conflicts between countries.

Building a federation

All these desirable and even noble objectives depend, however, on a Europe that is sufficiently united to be able to pursue them. That is why the Community must move towards becoming an effective federation that will have the capacity and authority matching those of the federations of the USA and the USSR. Of course the European federation will not be patterned on those of the other super-powers. Its development has different historical origins and its own distinct institutional system. The federal system that is emerging in Europe is likely to be much less centralized than that of many other federations. It is being formed by consent by independent and sovereign nation states that have agreed to pool and share their sovereignty in clearly defined spheres of activity. Federal devolution within most member states is gaining momentum in parallel.

The federal method can offer solutions to otherwise intractable internal conflicts such as, for instance, the language quarrels in Belgium which are now being resolved by the setting up of three autonomous regions under a federal constitution. Spain provides another example of the use of federal responses to the democratic demands for regional autonomy after the throttling centralism of the Franco fascist era. Effective self-government and autonomy for Gibraltar within Spain might ultimately be acceptable to its inhabitants provided that, as full citizens of a federal Europe, they would have their rights and autonomy guaranteed under the European constitution.

Might not a federal approach to the problems of Northern Ireland also offer some possible way out of the current impasse. Is it really beyond the wit of politicians to work out a system of autonomy and self-government for a province that would form part of an Irish federation while retaining a constitutional link with Britain? Is not such an approach likely, furthermore, to be more credible once both Ireland and Britain are full and equal member states within a European federation?

Such a European federation with functions and powers outlined above would require some reform of existing Community institutions. The first and foremost objective must be to correct the democratic deficit which has been highlighted by the Single European Act. Collective decisions of the Council of Ministers, especially when reached by majority, cannot be held accountable by twelve separate national parliaments. The European Parliament must acquire powers of co-decision with the Council in all spheres in order to give Community legislation democratic legitimacy.

The choice of European Commissioners, who in effect form the cabinet of an embryo European government, should not consist of nominees chosen or dismissed, often for idiosyncratic reasons, by national governments alone. Choice of his colleagues should be left to the President of the Commission in consultation with governments. At present he himself is chosen by the heads of governments for two-year terms. Moving towards the direct election of the President of the Commission by universal suffrage, for a term which corresponds to the term of the European Parliament, would have a number of advantages. It would considerably enhance public interest in European affairs and secure much higher participation in the European parliamentary elections.

This last suggestion for presidential elections highlights the whole issue of a distinct European identity; not one that replaces national, regional, or local loyalties, but one that builds a stronger sense of being part of Europe and its emerging federation. Many proposals to this end have been advanced by the Addonino Committee for a People's Europe, as described in chapter 6. Most of them have already been accepted by the Community institutions and many are being implemented. But the single most significant step in helping people to identify with Europe would be to enshrine in law a common European citizenship with clearly defined democratic rights and duties. The United States of Europe will never become a full reality until all its inhabitants feel themselves to be its citizens with a sense of belonging and a sense of loyalty towards it that is no weaker than that which they feel towards their nation, region or local community.

Shaping the future

If the case for the United States of Europe is a persuasive one, how is it actually to be brought about? On the face of it, decisions to transform the European Community into a full union lie first in the hands of national governments and then in those of national parliaments which have to ratify any major reforms proposed by their governments. Parliaments in our democratic societies have to take account of public opinion, which develops in response to many influences, with the media playing a powerful role and opinion formers including spokesmen of major interests, such as commerce, industry, and the trade unions, and by the politicians who form parliaments and governments. So the case for the United States of Europe needs to be made to governments and their parliaments against a background of a favourable trend of public opinion.

An examination of the history of the evolution of the European Community illustrates the process. First and foremost come the ideas. The objective of a European federation was already promoted in the 1920s by the Pan-Europe Union founded by the Austrian Count Coudenhove-Kalergi. His ideas and those of the founders of Federal Union were developed by the latter's Research Institute set up under the chairmanship of Sir William Beveridge in Oxford in 1939. Many distinguished academics and political thinkers contributed to the development of a wide-ranging body of literature on the theory of federalism and its application to post-war Europe. Others, not directly involved in Federal Union, shared their objectives and promoted them in their own way. Of those Jean Monnet was, without doubt, the foremost example.

The ideas and more detailed proposals for action were then communicated to political leaders who, once persuaded, were in a position to act. The first example of this was the proposal made by Winston Churchill, backed by his cabinet, to create a Franco-British Union in 1940. The key to this process of persuasion of politicians lies in a formula expressed by Monnet: 'Although much time is required to

147

attain power, only a small amount is required to explain to those who have it the way to solve actual difficulties ... when ideas are lacking, they accept yours with gratitude, on condition that you allow them to claim paternity. Because they run the risks, they have need of laurels.'

The political leaders of continental countries in exile in London and many in the resistance movements on the Continent during the war were much influenced and persuaded by the ideas of Federal Union and its publications. Many of them retained their commitment to a federal Europe after the war when they exercised positions of responsibility in their countries or in European forums. People like Paul Henri Spaak and Altiero Spinelli provide notable examples.

The ideas are of course communicated much more widely to opinion formers in all sectors of society who then spread the message amongst their peers and through them to their followers and public. Particularly important in this context are those who are behind the decision-makers, including civil servants and close political friends and supporters. The other key group consists of the journalists who can communicate the message to the wider public. The process of communication takes a variety of forms. Apart from the written word in books, pamphlets, and the media, conferences, seminars, and lectures provide the opportunity for verbal communication. The latter need not be confined to the issues to be promoted, but may well be introduced incidentally on platforms set up for discussion of other, though related topics. Then there are visible public demonstrations of support for the ideas which, by attracting media coverage, will in turn influence the politicians, who are always sensitive to public pressure.

Many of the ideas advanced in this book are those developed in much greater detail by experts in their respective subjects, who have undertaken research and participated in study groups and commissions set up to produce proposals for further progress in European integration. Foremost amongst these have been the study groups of the London based Federal Trust for Education and Research, which is the successor to William Beveridge's Federal Union Research Institute, and the Trans-European Policy Studies Association, set up by the Federal Trust and comprising authoritative research institutes in other European Community countries. Other proposals stem from the reports of commissions set up by the European Community institutions and from authoritative books on the subjects covered.

A number of the proposals, summarized here, have been disseminated widely and have already played a significant role in influencing opinion formers including politicians and their leaders throughout the Community. The process of continuous public education on European issues has over the years fallen to voluntary organizations such as the European Movement, operating in some fourteen European countries, and its individual membership organization the Union of European Federalists. Their role has been extensive and influential ever since their first combined Congress of Europe in the Hague in 1948 held under the chairmanship of Winston Churchill.

The European Movement, which is primarily an umbrella organization for all types of organizations with an interest in European affairs, keeps in touch with associations of individuals in every sector of society, This includes political parties, industry, commerce, trade unions, employers associations, most professions, educational establishments, and special interest organizations. The methods of disseminating ideas vary widely, from the organization of conferences and distribution of publications to the supply of speakers to address audiences of every variety from platforms provided by other organizations.

The Union of European Federalists consists of individual members within the European Movement and provides a valuable forum for its more active members, who discuss current European issues and plan public campaigns to promote their ideas. These may range from stimulating political parties and other organizations to focus their attention on European affairs, helping to raise public interest in European elections and organizing public demonstrations in favour of European unity. Amongst the latter, one of the most impressive took place during the 1985 Milan Summit meeting when close on 100,000 people from all over Europe took part. It has been said that, during the summit meeting, which argued about whether a conference should be convened to negotiate a new treaty for progress to Union, the Italian Premier turned on the television to show his colleagues the extent of public support for the idea.

Tactics for promoting European unification are various and complementary. Jean Monnet, who set up his Action Committee for the United States of Europe, relied on a small and carefully selected membership of political and trade union leaders to whom he submitted simple and concrete ideas that related to existing circumstances and could be put into effect relatively easily. His method was described as functional, and each step forward flowed from previous advances. Altiero Spinelli, one of the founders of the federalist movement, saw its role as one of persuading the wider public by promoting more populist but also longer term objectives. But both Monnet and Spinelli saw that the key to their success lay in persuading those with influence and power to their cause. Indeed, the latter's lasting monument to the cause was the blueprint for European Union, in the form of the Draft Treaty which he fathered and shepherded through to its adoption by a massive majority of the first elected European Parliament.

By giving a positive lead at the right time and in the right place, relatively few individuals can achieve major shifts in attitudes and persuade the decision-makers that their efforts will have general support. Time and time again, since the Second World War, committed Europeans have seen their efforts crowned with success. And success brings its own rewards to each active supporter: the feeling that, however humble their role, they will have contributed to shaping history. This is the motive for an ever swelling number of active protagonists for European unity. It is thanks to their efforts that a United States of Europe will surely come about.

A glimpse ahead

But what sort of Europe will it be? If progress towards a fully integrated single market by the end of 1992 is, according to the heads of the European Community's twelve member governments, irreversible, and Jacques Delors, President of the European Commission, was right in his 1988 claim that within ten years 80 per cent of economic legislation and maybe fiscal and social legislation will be of Community origin, then we will soon have an economic and monetary union with its own currency, directed by Community institutions. At the same time, NATO members of the European Community are strengthening and unifying the European pillar of the Atlantic Alliance through Western European Union and planning the progressive integration of their military forces. In the face of the gradual decline of US world dominance, the Europeans are developing their own political co-operation aimed at constructing a common foreign policy. These steps foreshadow a political union.

At the same time momentous changes are taking place within the Soviet bloc. Perestroika and democratization are introducing market principles and political pluralism, changing the Soviet system and bringing it closer to that enjoyed by the rest of Europe. The collapse of the communist system in central and eastern Europe and the adoption by most of the countries in the region of pluralist, democratic market economies as their objective have, in effect, ended the division of Europe into two ideologically incompatible blocs.

These dramatic changes have suddenly made the emergence, in the words of Winston Churchill, of a kind of United States of Europe that will include most European countries no longer a dream but a probable development. What will it be like to live in a United States of Europe? The following imaginary news story in one of Europe's newspapers of the year 2014 will, it is hoped, give an impression of the events and preoccupations likely at the time of a European Presidential Election.

Gabriella by a landslide

Brussels, 5 June 2014

At 11 a.m. the Chief Justice of the European Court formally declared Gabriella Bosconi re-elected President of the United States of Europe. He also confirmed the election of her two team mates, Vice-President Patrick Antrim, who will chair the Council of States, and Vice-President Krystyna Królik, who will preside over the European Parliament's Chamber of the People. The final results gave the three nominees of the Federal People's Party 51 per cent of the votes cast, and their main opponents, the centre right European Democrat candidates, 37 per cent. The candidates of the Associated National Parties were third with 11 per cent.

The final results were held up by power failures in Yugoslavia, which blacked out the transmission of votes to the central polling computer for several hours, and by inevitable delays in getting results transmitted from outlying Anatolian regions of Turkey, where voters had not yet been provided with personal transceivers with which to record their votes directly.

The four-week electoral campaign was dominated by the daily teleconferences which enabled hundreds of questions to be put to candidates by citizens from all the twenty-three member states of the Union, as well as by callers from other parts of the world. The issues which dominated the campaign were questions of national identity, conservation of the environment, relations with other world powers, and the promotion of global security.

Although the re-election of President Bosconi for a second term was never much in doubt, the extent of her victory was surprising. Political commentators attributed it partly to the shrewd choice of her two running mates. Patrick Antrim, the first protestant Taoiseach of the Irish Federation, brought to the ticket much respect gained from his successful negotiation of the re-unification of Ireland while allowing Ulster to retain a constitutional link with Britain. Krystyna Królik, who as Polish foreign minister had persuaded the Soviet government not to object to the accession of Poland, Czechoslovakia and Hungary to the United States of Europe, carried most of the eastern European states for her party.

Their principal opponents suffered from having fielded an all-male team. The nationalists, who came a poor third, failed to re-ignite the old campaign for the return of sovereign powers to the states, which were ceded to the Union under the 1998 constitution.

Interviewed by our correspondent after the declaration of the results, President Bosconi gave these answers to the questions put to her.

Q. Much was made during the campaign of the threat to national identity which, it was claimed, could only be safeguarded by the return of sovereign powers to the nation states. Why do you think the nationalists and their cause received such scant support?

Pres. Bosconi: The nationalists confused two distinct issues: the preservation of national cultures and languages and the return of sovereign powers to the states. The Union is committed to protecting and indeed enhancing the identity and integrity of its many nations, which so greatly enrich our common European heritage and culture. During my last administration over 2 billion Ecu were devoted to programmes protecting ethnic diversity and assisting the development of national cultural activities. We intend to spend even more in the coming years to further these aims. On the other hand the fully sovereign nation state is surely an anachronism in our interdependent world and most of the electors apparently understood the distinction between pride in one's nationality and state power. Our slogan of 'Unity with Diversity' carried the day.

Q. Does this mean that you see no future for the continued self-government of our member states?

Pres. B: On the contrary. After all, our constitution is based on the principle of subsidiarity, which means that the federal government can only exercise those responsibilities which cannot be more effectively dealt with at state, regional, or local level. That is why the Union's powers are confined to external and defence affairs, to overall economic and monetary management, and to the protection of our common environment. In the social sphere the bulk of the federal budget is directed towards reducing inequalities in wealth and living standards between the different regions of the Union. Whilst unfettered national sovereignty is now out of date, member states have full autonomy in raising and spending their own taxes. They retain their own legal and educational systems and responsibility for health and social security. Indeed they are responsible for all governmental activities not ceded to the Union or devolved to their regional or local authorities..

Q. Much concern was voiced during the campaign about the threat to our environment posed by the growing air pollution from the massive increase in road and air transport. What are your plans to deal with these problems?

Pres. B: As you know we intend to introduce legislation phasing out all internal combustion engines within the next five years and their replacement by the new battery powered electric motors. That will help to deal with air pollution. Easing road and air congestion will be much harder. I hope to form a Commission to examine the problems of traffic congestion and report to us within the next two years.

Q. To what do you attribute Europe's much improved relations with the Soviet Union and what are your hopes for future global security?

Pres. B: There is little doubt that the establishment twelve years ago of the Eurasian Energy and Environment Agency laid the foundations for the growing economic interdependence between our two Unions. War between us is now quite unthinkable in the light of the massive economic benefits we have both reaped from our co-operation.

On the question of global security, the agreement reached between the Soviet Union, the USA and ourselves to place all our nuclear weapons under the control of the World Security Authority so that it can deter any nuclear power from the threat or use of its weapons has, I believe, removed the spectre of nuclear holocaust from our planet. But now we need to build on that achievement. If war, nuclear or conventional, is to be permanently banished from our planet, then the time has come to plan for a world federation with a common government that would work for the well-being and greater prosperity of the whole of mankind. For this grand design the United States of Europe and the federations in other continents could provide the necessary blueprint.

Appendix

PRINCIPAL FEDERALIST ORGANIZATIONS

Federal Union
Federal Trust for Education and Research
(British member of the network of the Trans-European Studies
Association)
The European Movement (British Council)

1 Whitehall Place, London, SW1A 2DA

————

Union of European Federalists
(with national, regional, and local organizations in seventeen
countries)
The European Movement
(international organization, with National Councils
in fourteen countries)

Rue du Trône 98, B-1050 Bruxelles, Belgium

————

Association to Unite the Democracies

1506, Pennsylvania Avenue SE, Washington DC 20003, USA

————

World Association for World Federation

Leliegracht 21, 1016 GR Amsterdam, The Netherlands

Bibliography

Albert, M. and Ball, J. (1983) *Towards European Recovery in the 1980s*, Luxembourg: The European Parliament.

Angell, N. (1933) *The Great Illusion*, London: William Heinemann.

Boyd Orr, J. (1940) 'Federalism and Science' in Channing-Pearce, M. (ed.) *Federal Union*, London: Jonathan Cape.

Budd, A. (1987) *The EEC – A Guide to the Maze*, 2nd edn, London: Kogan Page.

Burrows, B., Denton, G., and Edwards, G. (eds) (1978) *Federal Solutions to European Issues*, London: Macmillan.

Butler, M. (1986) *Europe – More than a Continent*, London: Heinemann.

Cecchini, P. (1988) *The European Challenge 1992*, Aldershot: Wildwood House.

Coudenhove-Kalergi, R. (1966) *Pan-Europa*, 3rd edn, Vienna: Pan-Europa Verlag.

EC Commission (1970) *Economic and Monetary Union* (Werner Report), Luxembourg: EC Bulletin.

—— (1970) *Problems of Political Unification* (Davignon Report), Luxembourg: EC Bulletin.

—— (1976) *European Union* (Tindemans Report), Luxembourg: EC Bulletin.

—— (1977) *Role of Public Finance on European Integration* (MacDougall Report), Brussels: European Communities.

—— (1977) *Treaties establishing the European Communities*, abridged version, Luxembourg: European Communities.

—— (1981) *Draft European Act* (Genscher-Colombo Report), Luxembourg: EC Bulletin.

—— (1985a) *A People's Europe* (Adonnino Report), Luxembourg: European Communities.

—— (1985b) *Completing the Internal Market* (Cockfield White Paper), Luxembourg: European Communities.

—— (1986) *Single European Act*, Luxembourg: EC Bulletin.

—— (1987) *A Strategy for the Evolution of the Economic System of the EC* (Padoa-Schioppa Report), Brussels: European Communities.

—— (1990) *The Community Charter of Fundamental Social Rights for Workers*, Luxembourg: European Communities.

European Parliament (1984) *Draft Treaty establishing the European Union*, Luxembourg: European Parliament.

Heath, E. (1988) *European Unity over the Next Ten Years: from Community to Union* (Lothian Memorial Lecture), London: Royal Institute of International Affairs.

Hoggart, R. and Johnson, D. (1987) *An Idea of Europe*, London: Chatto & Windus.

Layton, C. (1986) *One Europe: One World*, London: Journal of World Trade Law.

—— (1989) *A Step Beyond Fear*, London: Federal Trust for Education and Research.

Leonard, D. (1988) *Pocket Guide to the European Community*, Oxford: Basil Blackwell.

Lipgens, W. (1986) *Documents on the History of European Integration*, New York: Walter de Gruyter.

Mayne, R. and Pinder, J. with Roberts, J. (forthcoming) *A History of Federal Union*, London: Macmillan.

Monnet, J. (1976) *Memoirs*, trans. R. Mayne (1978), London: William Collins.

Pelkmans, J. and Winters, A. (1988) *Europe's Domestic Market*, London: Routledge.

Pryce, R. (ed.) (1987) *The Dynamics of European Union*, London: Croom Helm.

Robbins, L. (1939) *The Economic Causes of War*, London: Jonathan Cape.

Royal Institute of International Affairs (1988) *Europe's Future in Space*, London: Routledge & Kegan Paul.

Sharp, M. and Shearman, C. (1987) *European Technological Cooperation*, London: Routledge & Kegan Paul.

Vandamme, J. (ed.) (1985) *New Dimensions in European Social Policy*, London: Croom Helm.

Vile, M.J.C. (1973) *Federalism in the United States, Canada and Australia*, Research Papers 2, Commission on the Constitution, London: HMSO.

Index